THE 78 BIGGEST MISTAKES NEW MANAGERS MAKE

WHAT YOU NEED TO KNOW TO AVOID CAREER SUICIDE

Marjorie K. Treu

Love Your Life Publishing
Dallastown, PA

78 BIGGEST MISTAKES NEW MANAGERS MAKE
What You Need to Know to Avoid Career Suicide

Copyright © 2010 Marjorie K. Treu

All rights reserved. No part of this book may be reproduced or transmitted in any form or by any means, electronic or mechanical including photography, recording or any information storage and retrieval system without written permission from the author.

Published by:
Love Your Life Publishing
PO Box 2, Dallastown, PA 17313
(800) 930-3713

ISBN: 978-0-9820477-4-3
Library of Congress Control No: 2010938953
Cover design, layout and typesetting by Josiah Werning
Editing Coach: Rochelle Melander

Printed in the United States of America

To Denise and Mark, Lesa and George, Karen and Bruce for allowing me to develop my leadership skills over the years – forgiving the mistakes and helping me to discover myself in the process.

TABLE OF CONTENTS

- 6   About the Author
- 7   Acknowledgements
- 9   Introduction

- 13   Mistake #1 – *Let Your Ego Run Wild*
- 14   Mistake #2 – *Change Everything Immediately*
- 15   Mistake #3 – *Pretend You Know It All*
- 16   Mistake #4 – *Don't Build Trust Quickly*
- 17   Mistake #5 – *Micromanage the Team*
- 18   Mistake #6 – *Don't Get Yourself a Coach*
- 19   Mistake #7 – *Waste Your Boss's Time*
- 20   Mistake #8 – *Spend Too Much Time with Under-Performers*
- 21   Mistake #9 – *Have a Cloudy Vision*
- 22   Mistake #10 – *Avoid Goal Setting*
- 23   Mistake #11 – *Think You Don't Need a Mentor*
- 24   Mistake #12 – *Don't Pay Attention to Employee Morale*
- 25   Mistake #13 – *Don't Communicate Well*
- 26   Mistake #14 – *Afraid to Do Anything*
- 27   Mistake #15 – *Avoid Your Critics*
- 28   Mistake #16 – *Avoid Responsibility*
- 29   Mistake #17 – *Under-estimate the Value of Feedback*
- 30   Mistake #18 – *Show Disrespect*
- 31   Mistake #19 – *Give Vague Expectations*
- 32   Mistake #20 – *Meeting Mayhem*
- 33   Mistake #21 – *Avoid Conflict*
- 34   Mistake #22 – *Unable to Give Presentations*
- 35   Mistake #23 – *Forget Promises*
- 36   Mistake #24 – *Hire Only for Personality*
- 37   Mistake #25 – *Dodge Personal Openness*
- 38   Mistake #26 – *Do It All Yourself*
- 39   Mistake #27 – *Forget Email is Public*
- 40   Mistake #28 – *Take Action Slowly*
- 41   Mistake #29 – *Lack Confidence*
- 42   Mistake #30 – *Procrastination*
- 43   Mistake #31 – *Don't Protect Your Team*
- 44   Mistake #32 – *Ignore Personal Loss*
- 45   Mistake #33 – *Give Orders*
- 46   Mistake #34 – *Show Favoritism*
- 47   Mistake #35 – *Talk Down to People*
- 48   Mistake #36 – *Don't Network Enough*
- 49   Mistake #37 – *Forget Rewards*
- 50   Mistake #38 – *Don't Deal with Outbursts*
- 51   Mistake #39 – *Ignore the Unwritten Rules*
- 52   Mistake #40 – *Become Exclusive Too Quickly*

Page	Title
53	Mistake #41 – *Don't Understand Team Roles/Responsibilities*
55	Mistake #42 – *Sloppy Decision-Making*
57	Mistake #43 – *Fear Overload*
58	Mistake #44 – *Ignore Professional Development*
59	Mistake #45 – *Ungratefulness*
60	Mistake #46 – *Allow Negativity*
61	Mistake #47 – *Hide in Your Office*
62	Mistake #48 – *Constantly Put Out Fires*
63	Mistake #49 – *Play Politics*
64	Mistake #50 – *Under-Develop the Whole Team*
65	Mistake #51 – *Forget to Manage Upwards*
66	Mistake #52 – *Create a Demotivating Environment*
67	Mistake #53 – *Think Your Image Doesn't Matter*
69	Mistake #54 – *Burnout*
70	Mistake #55 – *Have an Outdated Resume*
71	Mistake #56 – *Don't Lead Through a Crisis*
72	Mistake #57 – *Bad Habits*
73	Mistake #58 – *Don't Build a Team Identity*
74	Mistake #59 – *Need to be Right*
75	Mistake #60 – *Ethical Dilemmas*
77	Mistake #61 – *Always Be Serious*
78	Mistake #62 – *Be a Rogue Leader*
79	Mistake #63 – *Pomposity*
80	Mistake #64 – *Lack of Self Management*
82	Mistake #65 – *Perfectionism*
83	Mistake #66 – *Don't Involve Staff Regularly*
84	Mistake #67 – *Manipulate*
85	Mistake #68 – *Don't Create a Life Plan*
87	Mistake #69 – *Over-Reliance on Technology*
88	Mistake #70 – *Untimely Performance Reviews*
89	Mistake #71 – *Don't Deal with Difficult People*
90	Mistake #72 – *Tell Everyone You're In Charge*
91	Mistake #73 – *Think You Can Manage Friends*
92	Mistake #74 – *Be Efficient vs. Effective*
93	Mistake #75 – *Inability to Refuse Employee Requests*
94	Mistake #76 – *Don't Expect the Dark Side of Management*
95	Mistake #77 – *Resist Change*
96	Mistake #78 – *Stay Too Late at the "Party"*
98	Afterword: What Comes Next?
100	Workshops and Teambuilding Events
101	Coaching/Mentoring Program
103	Keynote Speeches

ABOUT THE AUTHOR

After working in corporate America for over 20 years, Marjorie Treu began a consulting practice specializing in helping managers with team leadership issues. Her experience with Fortune 500 companies and small businesses in the travel, banking, retail, and manufacturing industries revealed the need to concisely bring the "how to" of managing people quickly into a manager's hand.

Marjorie is an inspirational management coach and engaging speaker who provides training, workshops, lectures, and coaching to hundreds of managers throughout the United States.

Her most popular programs include Adventures in Leadership, Management Makeover Workshops, and VIP Team Coaching Days. Her insights and articles are regularly published in her free bi-weekly Team Talk Today ezine. For more information, visit www.TeamFusion.net today.

Marjorie holds a B.S. in Education from the University of Wisconsin-Milwaukee and earned her PHR (Professional in Human Resources) certification through the Society of Human Resources Management. Additionally, she has served on the Board of the Southeast Wisconsin chapter of the American Society of Training & Development (ASTD) and volunteered with Junior Achievement.

Leaving Chicago after 20 years, Marjorie returned to her Milwaukee hometown for a decade before settling in Atlanta. She is currently being trained by her miniature schnauzers, Sadie and Sasha.

ACKNOWLEDGEMENTS

No book is ever written in a vacuum. It takes the input and wisdom of many people for it to come together in a meaningful way. I could not have completed this book without the help of extraordinary individuals. Individuals who contributed to the actual book production, and all those who kept me sane during the process.

To the Contributors: Penny Romasko, Karen T, Marsha Burger, Kit Behling, Marla Holman, Marge Foster, and Anonymous (you know who you are) for your willingness to expose your biggest mistake so others can learn from your experience. You are brave. And, to all those behind-the-scenes who shared privately so their current employers' reputation would be preserved.

To Rochelle Melander: My deepest gratitude for the time you spent coaching me from idea conception through revisions. Your writing coaching has been invaluable. I'm grateful for the day I was introduced to your work through: www.WriteNowCoach.com.

To Josiah Werning: For using your awesome design abilities to visually capture the essence of my message. You have such remarkable talent and spirit. I thank God for the work he is doing through you. I encourage everyone to visit www.JosiahWerning.com to witness your diversity.

To Bruce and Karen: For offering me the freedom to create, the solace of friendship, the gift of acceptance, and the refuge of a nurturing home. I promise – no more puppies! Thank you for loving Sadie and Sasha like your own. It means the world to me.

INTRODUCTION

Over the years, I've trained and coached hundreds of managers as they have stepped into a new management role. These talented people were usually promoted or hired based on excellent technical skills. The majority of these new managers struggled in finding the balance between learning company policies and products or services and managing their own team. Where they originally had great success they were now fighting to perform well in a new environment.

In their haste to make a good impression, they focused only on understanding company culture and the customer. What they neglected was connecting first with their own work group. They didn't build a team of people who supported each other. They didn't take time to build rapport, establish guidelines, and work through difficulties. Often, they neglected their group so long that problems started infiltrating the group. Issues occurred, such as:

- Increased tardiness and absenteeism
- Low morale
- High employee turnover
- Gossip and rumors among staff members
- More employee grievances to the Human Resources department
- Greater incidents of customer complaints
- Little participation in staff meetings and office events

Are you faced with any of these situations? Then settle in because there is good news and bad news. Let's start with the bad news because it has to do with you as a manager. This may seem harsh especially since I don't know anything about your ability to lead.

The Bad News – You are responsible for the state of your staff and your career. Employees look to their manager for direction, and if you have not provided conscious and consistent direction then trouble will follow.

The Good News – It's not too late! You can learn to be better if you take to heart the biggest mistakes new managers make and not fall victim to them. This book helps you navigate the worst mistakes.

How to Use This Book

Rather than reading through tons of material, you can save time and energy by simply reviewing the Table of Contents and choosing the chapters you would like to focus on. You can read *78 Biggest Mistakes New Managers Make* in short segments or skip around depending on where you need the most help.

In about 5-minutes, you will get an overview of The Mistake and real-world, practical advice on overcoming that obstacle. Isn't that time investment worth the pay-off in employee goodwill and higher customer satisfaction levels?

What You Will Find in This Book

Continue reading and discover:

- What to do when managing employees.
- Mistakes made by dozens of managers, and tips on what they did to recover.
- FREE checklists to save you time.
- Four BONUS e-books.
- Supplemental information to jump-start your learning.

Imagine how different your work life could be 30-days from now; how you fast-track your career over the next 2 years…

It's up to you. Choose to design your success. Decide to be great!

Marjorie

Disclaimer:
This book is not intended to replace legal advice or to be a substitute for seeking guidance from your Human Resources department.
Your due diligence is required.

the mistakes

MISTAKE 1 – *LET YOUR EGO RUN WILD*

You have worked hard and now earned a promotion. Along with that comes a new job title and office. Maybe you've been waiting for this for years while colleagues or friends have passed you by. Congratulations!

But, how you became a manager has little to do with how well you will perform in your new role. Success looks different as a manager than it did as a worker. The sooner you recognize that fact, the better off you'll be.

We all have Egos. They are what make you want authority, status, recognition for accomplishments, and what gives you confidence. Yet, EGO can lay a path of destruction from poor communication to faulty decision making.
The obnoxious and overbearing behavior that comes with the ego's activity can damage creativity, undermine effective problem-solving, and cause stress.

You'll know when your Ego is rearing its ugly head when you notice yourself:
- Taking credit for every idea.
- Dominating conversations and meetings.
- Interrupting other people who are expressing their ideas.
- Telling others of your superiority whether real or perceived.
- Almost always using "I" and "me" in conversation.

TIPS:
- Allow others to speak first and express their opinion.
- Mentally count how many times you say "I" or "me" during a conversation. Ask yourself, "Do I honestly have better ideas than the other person, so I don't listen to them?"

MISTAKE #2 – *CHANGE EVERYTHING IMMEDIATELY*

The pace of CHANGE is increasing rapidly. You may have been brought to the position to make sweeping changes or not. Regardless, you need to put thought into:

- What kind of change is necessary to get better results.
- Who needs to be involved with the change.
- What happens if I don't agree with the team members change idea.
- Who will be affected by the change.
- What is the best timing for the change to occur.
- What is the right way to communicate the need for change and why.
- What is the rate of adjustments I'm asking from the team.
- How easily will the team take in and use new information.

"I've been running the Expo for years and have a wonderful team of volunteers who are dedicated to the cause," said Penny Romasko, Executive Director of The Great Lakes Pet Expo, Milwaukee, WI. "The majority of our success comes from the creative ideas from the PR and Entertainment committees.

Every September, I invite the Committee Chairs to a kickoff planning meeting for the next year, and ask them to bring a proposed budget and their committees' plan. One year, the PR Committee proposed eliminating what I believed was our best marketing idea because they felt the cost was too high. I didn't want to dismiss their idea and was 100% uncomfortable with the change.

At the wrap-up meeting, we discovered that attendance was down by 2,200 people from the previous year. That is significant to the amount of money donated back to pet rescue. Unfortunately, we made three major changes that year. I have no evidence which of the changes caused the drop in attendance."

TIPS:
- Don't reinvent the wheel. Just because something isn't done your way does not necessarily mean it's wrong. Learn the difference between "different" and "wrong."
- To more accurately track results of changes, make only one change at a time. If you make multiple changes simultaneously, you won't be able to tell from the data collected which of the changes had the most impact.

MISTAKE 3 – *PRETEND YOU KNOW IT ALL*

New managers are often under the misconception that they need to know everything. The reality is that you do not. You were offered the job because your skills and abilities were the best match to the job description, not the perfect match. Recruiters spend time doing due diligence in verifying your qualifications and experience and pass that information along to your new boss.

Your boss won't expect you to know every aspect of the job on day one. Most companies provide new employees both formal and on-the-job training. If someone asks you a question and you don't know the answer, it's acceptable to say, "Let me find out."

It's far better to confess you don't know something than try to bluff your way through… even if you need to admit your lack of knowledge every day for weeks before your learning curve is over.

TIPS:
- Find out from your boss his or her top three priorities for your first 30-days on the job. Get the training you need if you are not well-versed on the topic.
- Informally, ask your staff what they believe your top priorities are. If they are different than your boss, it is a good time to have an open discussion on what you will be spending your time working on the first 30-, 60-, and 90-days on the job.

MISTAKE 4 – *DON'T BUILD TRUST QUICKLY*

It begins with you. (I know you're not surprised.)

Leaders need to promote and sustain a general feeling of "we are all in this together" in order to foster a climate of collaboration among team members. But, how do you actually do this when you are new to a team?

Simply, trust means confidence. The opposite (distrust) is suspicion. When you trust people, you have confidence in them – in their integrity and in their abilities.

Ideally, building trust and confidence should be the initial focus of any relationship as you get to know team members. Building trust is foundational in helping the team move forward as you work through issues, and time well spent as the relationship moves forward.

TIPS:
- Be honest and let people know where you stand.
- Apologize quickly if you are wrong and make things right.
- Be first to extend trust to others – extend it freely to those who have earned your trust; extend it conditionally to those who are earning your trust.

MISTAKE 5 – *MICROMANAGE THE TEAM*

Listen up: You are not the center of the universe! A recent statistic noted that nearly 8 in 10 employees are victims of a micro-managing boss.

Do any of these statements sound familiar?
1. I can do a team member's job more efficiently than they can.
2. I frequently "check in" with team members and offer comments, both positive and negative, on how the work is progressing.
3. I rarely see the "big picture" because I'm trying to control everyone else's moves.

If this sounds like you, it's a pretty good bet that your management style is being described by your employees as micro-management. Unfortunately, it is not a complimentary term. A micro-manager monitors and assesses employee performance and progress every step of the way. Simply put, micro-managers are managers that oversee their team too closely. They are constantly looking over shoulders and making unwarranted remarks.

How do you know if you micro-manage? If you are asking yourself this question, then something has happened to give you the idea you may be exhibiting the behavior.

Further hints that you may be micro-managing:
1. Team members say less.
2. Conversations end abruptly when you are near.
3. Your perception is that everything is under control (actually, it's not).
4. Dialogue seems awkward between you and the team.
5. The team is not offering solutions.

TIPS:
- Ask a question and listen without interrupting.
- Do not offer an answer. Have the team figure out the solution. If you are uncertain what they are suggesting, keep prompting them by asking for clarity.

MISTAKE 6 – *DON'T GET YOURSELF A COACH*

In addition to all your other job responsibilities, the prospect of coaching can be overwhelming. First, the topic is huge in scope. Second, it takes time to provide coaching. Coaching boils down to three things your team needs from you on a day-to-day basis:
1. They need to be inspired.
2. They need to be encouraged.
3. They need to be challenged.

How do you become this great coach for your team? By being coachable yourself. Find and work with the right coach to help you strengthen those areas where you need additional skills.

You and your coach need to set aside formal time to update your progress. It can be a quick 10-minute check-in using the following questions:
1. How do you think you are doing?
2. In what areas do you need to improve?
3. What are your goals in the next 1-2 weeks?

Your relationship with a leadership coach should be open, honest, and make it safe for you to fail. The concept of "failing" is tough because of the stigma attached to business failure. You need to ask yourself, "To what extent do I allow myself to fail in order to learn? What is an acceptable loss to the company?" Handle your failures in a positive and professional way.

TIPS:
- Be open to receive ongoing coaching without thinking of it as a sign of weakness.
- Not all advice is good advice. Look for trends in your behavior before making changes. If you are hearing the same thing from many people, that is a good indicator there is truth in their observations. Evaluate their comments in context to the whole situation versus honing in on only one incident.
- Further your development with the Team Fusion COACHING/MENTORING Program (Continuing Education Enrollment Form in back of book on page 101). Your company's Tuition Reimbursement Program may underwrite this investment.

MISTAKE 7 – *WASTE THE TIME OF YOUR BOSS*

I know you are intelligent and have figured out that your #1 working relationship is with… **YOUR BOSS.**

Your boss can:
1. Be your advocate or worst nightmare.
2. Make what you experience inside an organization one of value or not.
3. Influence how quickly you are promoted.

You may think that your boss understands how busy you are and won't need any of your time. Get that thought out of your head! Your job is to help your boss. You may represent only 1% of his or her problems, don't make it as if it is 100%.

Yes, you have preoccupations, problems to solve and issues to tackle. However, while your time is entirely devoted to them, do not expect your boss's time to be also.

TIPS:
- Budget time to meet with him or her to both give and receive information, guidance, and training. As a new hire, have meetings more frequently so your boss gets to know you and your management style. The frequency of meetings can be adjusted over time based on workload and availability.
- Come to each meeting prepared to discuss project updates, challenges, customer and staff situations, and what went well. Don't put yourself in a position of needing to come back with information because you forgot to bring it to the discussion.
- The more simple the problem or issue at hand, the less time you should have him or her spend on it: prepare, summarize, and synthesize information and options. Do not confuse your more frequent problems with the most important ones.
- Book several meetings in advance. Nothing is more frustrating than to have to wait days, weeks or months for that extra new meeting needed in order to finalize a decision or a project.

MISTAKE 8 – *SPEND TOO MUCH TIME WITH UNDER-PERFORMERS*

Under-performing employees present a difficult challenge for managers. How you respond can determine whether a problem is quickly resolved or becomes an even larger issue.

You may need to terminate the employee, but that should not be your first thought, and isn't necessarily the best option.

Try these techniques:
1. Take immediate action. You do not need to wait for the employee's review to discuss poor performance.
2. Schedule a private meeting to talk about the issue(s) you see. The employee must know what they are doing wrong in order to be able to change.
3. Your conversation must be two-way. Give your employee the opportunity to respond to your concerns.
4. Document, document, document.
5. Collaboratively, create an improvement plan outlining specific steps and a timeline for completion.
6. If possible, assign a mentor with strong interpersonal and coaching skills and an enthusiastic attitude.
7. Periodically check-in with the employee before the deadline on his or her improved performance. Let them know how they are progressing and if the changes they have made are meeting your expectations.

TIPS:
- When considering termination as an option make sure the consequence matches the severity of the situation consistently with the entire organization (not just your department). Human Resources is your best advocate in these situations.
- A performance improvement plan is considered a "formal warning" in many organizations. Do not take it lightly.

MISTAKE 9 – *HAVE A CLOUDY VISION*

> *"Good business leaders create a vision, articulate the vision, passionately own the vision, and relentlessly drive it to completion."*
> *- Jack Welch*

What is the importance of visioning? **Visioning** is what it says - creating a very clear future. It describes, in full emotional detail, the way it will be in the future when your business, team and even life are just how you want them. So this can be applied in any area of your life and business. Visioning is of huge importance in the workplace today.

Visioning is foundational to your leadership. You need to be clear about the vision for yourself, your team, and your organization. Working within this context, you will be able to give clarity to the choices and decisions you make. A corporate vision statement, much like your personal one, is the guiding light of inspiring words chosen by successful leaders to clearly and concisely convey the direction of the organization. Clear mission and vision statements communicate your intentions and motivate your team to realize a common vision of the future.

TIPS:
- Write out your personal vision statement for the team. Then, communicate the direction you are heading.
- Write your vision statement as an aspiration of the future.
- Identify what you, your customers and other stakeholders will value most about how your department contributes to achieve the organization's mission.

MISTAKE 10 – *AVOID GOAL SETTING*

Planning is all about being prepared – looking ahead and listing the tasks to be completed, identifying needed resources, providing any needed training, and anticipating any problems that could arise. Some benefits of planning include:
- Team members can coordinate their work to recognize if potential scheduling conflicts exist.
- Sequencing of deadlines so the overall project is finished by the due date.
- A sense of direction to team members by giving the global picture.

Why don't more managers set goals and plan? Simply, it takes time up front. At a minimum, a well developed plan should include these 5 essential sections:
1. List of tasks and sequencing of these activities.
2. Identify all resources – budget, vendors, additional staff.
3. Recognize all stakeholders.
4. Determine standards for outcomes, results, and review.
5. Analyze possible problems.

You, as the new manager, need to take responsibility to initiate the planning process and update the plan as work progresses. It will save time if you create the first plan draft and present the project scope and plan to your team. Get input from the team prior to creating the actual plan for distribution. While you think you may have captured all the elements, the team will be able to provide greater detail based on their area of specialty.

TIPS:
- Does each person know what to do and why they're doing it?
- Do individual goals align with the business goals?
- Are goals written in a SMART (Specific, Measurable, Attainable, Realistic, Timebound – see Mistake #19) format so people can both understand and apply them to their daily work?

MISTAKE 11 – *THINK YOU DON'T NEED A MENTOR*

Serious leaders never enter a mentoring relationship with the expectation of failure. In fact, the opposite is true – you expect tremendous results because you admire and respect the person. You have selected them because of their achievements, and want to emulate their success.

Reasons Why You Need a Mentor:
- Someone unbiased to be accountable to. As your career progresses, it's easy to fall victim to the "I'm at the top and can take it easy" trap. Your mentor won't let you rest on past laurels. He or she makes sure you complete shared goals, and doesn't allow recurring postponement of tasks.
- Someone to help you refine your ideas/approach and put them into practice. You have ideas but the day isn't long enough to implement them all. Your mentor can help sift through the viable ideas and coach you around marginal ones.
- Someone who has more ideas than you for growth development. Your mentor looks at all facets of your development – interpersonal, emotional, technical, social, etc – to help you understand principles for a successful business life.
- Someone that has contacts you need. There will come a time when you outgrow your current network. Your mentor has additional contacts and knows where to find information you seek.

TIPS:
- Set expectations at the beginning of the relationship as to how long you expect to be mentored.
- Ending a formal mentoring relationship does not signal the need to end a friendship. Separate business from personal.

MISTAKE 12 – *DON'T PAY ATTENTION TO EMPLOYEE MORALE*

I'm often asked, "How do I motivate someone?" as if there was a magic answer lurking in the universe. If only it were that simple! The field of psychology has studied human behavior and used the word "motivation" to refer to the reasons someone engages in a particular behavior. The fact is that every person is motivated – either positively or negatively – from within themselves.

A wise manager will not assume that every team member shares the same needs in the workplace. The best you can do is shape the work environment to allow employees to bring out their best effort and be motivated about work priorities. *Here is how:*

- **The power of an employee survey.** This can be as formal as a written survey or focus groups, but the most effective method is simply talking to team members every single day.
- **Minimize rules and policies.** Write only the minimum number of rules and policies needed to legally protect your organization. Then, develop guidelines that interpret the rules and policies in a fair and consistent manner by everyone.
- **Talk, talk, then talk some more.** Use multiple methods to clearly communicate work place guidelines and department expectations for professional behavior.
- **Involve your team.** People like to control their work so allow them to help set their individual goals, give input into decisions, visually track their progress, and create team incentives.
- **Provide personal development opportunities.** Keep employees engaged by offering personal development growth through education, training, job sharing, team participation, cross-training, and job shadowing.

Rewards and recognition work. You need to tap into the intrinsic motivation of each person and provide rewards and recognition that appeal to them individually.

TIPS:
- Take 3 minutes at the start of your next team meeting to do a quick brainstorm. The best ideas will come from your team.
- Give employees exactly what they like as rewards by visiting www.78ManagerMistakes.com. Click on FREE RESOURCES tab and download the *My Favorites* form.

MISTAKE 13 – *DON'T COMMUNICATE WELL*

If you surveyed employees and asked them what their top challenges at work are, the answer "communication" would appear near the top of the list. It does nearly every time. It's even more of a challenge the larger your organization.

Interaction between people is the basis of communication. Words, sound, speaking, and language are some of the key components that make up verbal communication. Communication develops not from words alone, but the meaning people put into the words.

As a manager, it's your responsibility to eliminate misunderstanding through speaking directly with someone. The frustrating thing is managers make these assumptions:
- Talking indicates your message is as important to staff as it is to you.
- Your message is clear.
- People like you enough to listen and learn.
- The language you use relates to all people.

Yes, your organization values your knowledge and experience but it also counts on you to understand interpersonal dynamics. A leader who struggles with low morale, high absenteeism, and increasing turnover is probably a leader who has failed to truly listen to the needs and concerns of their team.

A new manager especially needs to **listen** more than speak those first critical months on the job.

TIPS:
- Best communication tip given to me by a mentor is: Think before you speak or write!
- Receive more in-depth information on verbal, nonverbal and written communication with special sections on listening and presentations. For your complimentary copy of the e-book, *Team Leadership Essentials: The Art of Communication* visit www.78ManagerMistakes.com. Click on the FREE RESOURCES tab and download *Art of Communication* ebook.

MISTAKE 14 – *AFRAID TO DO ANYTHING*

Unusual as it is, you may be a manager who did not ask for the promotion. You came to work one day, and the job was handed to you. Maybe you aren't sure you can do the job.

This is exactly what happened early in my travel career at Going Places in Lake Geneva, IL.

A few months after being hired as a travel agent there was a meeting between the agency owners and the manager. After the meeting, the manager left the building and the two owners called me into my boss's office.

They told me that the manager no longer worked there, and they were naming me the agency's new manager. It was one of those "slow motion" moments. I remember looking at their beaming faces and thinking, "They look like they've just handed me the keys to the city." I did not have the same feeling.

There is a huge gap between sitting in the manager's office, and actually functioning as one. My biggest mistake was letting the feeling of inadequacy shut me down to the point of inactivity. I didn't know what I didn't know. So, I did very little of the new job for weeks afterwards.

TIPS:
- Remember, upper management would not have put you into the job if they didn't believe you could handle it.
- Find out what your manager expects you to do (which may be different than your job description), and learn those skills quickly.

MISTAKE 15 – *AVOID YOUR CRITICS*

As the saying goes, "You can please some people all of the time, and you can please all people some of the time, but you can't please all people all of the time!" This is true for life in general but becomes more apparent when you land in a leadership role.

You will find a couple people you can please all the time, a few you can please some of the time, and many you won't please at all -- regardless of how much you listen and empathize.

Whether you're a team member, peer, colleague, coach, or leader… you WILL be criticized. The more popular you get, the bigger your circle of influence becomes, the more visible you are, the more criticism you will receive.

Just because you have risen to a leadership position does not automatically grant you the super power of being immune to critics. Even the best manager will encounter team members who:
- Misunderstand your intentions.
- Misinterpret your instructions.
- Criticize anyone in management.

There will be days that you simply cannot ignore critical remarks. They may be nasty and aimed directly at you. They may be someone just venting. They may be unfounded. But, when someone is confronting and criticizing you what can you do?

3 Steps to Diffusing Your Critics:

Step 1 – Respond calmly and acknowledge their viewpoint.
Step 2 – Track trends.
Step 3 – Always follow up.

TIPS:
- Be honest with yourself. If three people say the same thing about you, there is a good chance it is true. Find out if there is truth in their observation.
- If the criticism is blatantly false, just let it go.

MISTAKE 16 – *AVOID RESPONSIBILITY*

Like it or not, as the manager you are responsible for everything that happens in your group, whether you did it, or knew about it, or not. Anything anyone in your group does, or doesn't do, reflects on you. You have to build the communications so there are no surprises, but also be prepared to shoulder the responsibility.

The word "accountability" has been thrown around for years yet few understand what it takes to be accountable. The easiest explanation of accountability I've heard comes from *Accountability That Works* by CRM Films. According to CRM, Accountability consists of three phases:

1. RESPONSIBILITY – A before-the-fact mindset of ownership for a task or job.

- Make a clear agreement and write it down.
- Identify the benefits of completing the task.
- Avoid the "We Syndrome" (every task has an owner).

2. EMPOWERMENT – Taking personal action in order to ensure an agreed upon result.

- Decide on the needed steps to be taken.
- Ask for assistance (if needed).
- Overcome barriers – You may not have decision authority, but you do have the power to ask questions and find out..

3. ACCOUNTABILITY – Personal willingness, after-the-fact, to answer for the results of your behaviors and actions (regardless of how things turned out).

- Review, "Did I complete each step of my agreement?"
- Take responsibility for fixing the problem.
- Learn from your experience (so you'll do it better next time).

TIPS:
- Listen to all sides on a project update before speaking. Seek to understand before diagnosing.
- Hold yourself, as well as others, accountable by taking responsibility for all results.

MISTAKE 17 – *UNDER-ESTIMATE THE VALUE OF FEEDBACK*

Feedback – who needs it? We all do.

Managers who give feedback skillfully and tactfully help the team improve skills and grow professionally. People who listen to feedback openly correct mistakes sooner and improve work methods more quickly. The key to feedback is to give and receive it on a daily basis.

TIPS:
- Start your sentences either with "I" or with a direct statement of the problem.
- Give feedback as close to the event as possible. Your memory will be clearer.
- Don't give negative feedback if the person is feeling especially pressured.
- Be in emotional control when giving feedback.
- Praise in public, criticize in private.
- When you want someone to listen and learn keep your voice neutral, speak in normal conversational tones, and avoid sounding angry.
- Your goal is to build the relationship with your team member. Give sincere compliments, use friendly courtesies, and offer assistance.
- Empathize – put yourself in the other person's position.
- Pinpoint Problems – be very specific by sticking to the facts. Take the time to determine what's wrong and what you're asking for.
- Move Forward. With your team, you can give instructions, assignments, or orders. With peers and superiors, you move forward by opening a discussion or a negotiation.

MISTAKE 18 – *SHOW DISRESPECT*

You are probably familiar with The Golden Rule: Treat others as you want to be treated. What happens when we do not treat other human beings with respect?

A culture of disrespect becomes evident in the workplace. These are conscious or unconscious learned behaviors that show you do not care that other people are human beings.

Disrespectful behaviors include:

1. Causing pain and suffering.
2. Devaluing the person and their ideas.
3. Trivializing individual accomplishments.
4. Not listening to the person.
5. Excluding someone from team conversations.
6. Feeling isolated which creates low morale.

As disrespect increases you will notice discrimination, stereotyping, harassment, and bullying become more prevalent.

RESPECT FORMULA

SHOWING (behaviors + words) + **REGARD** (recognition) + **for OTHERS** (human beings) = **RESPECT**

TIPS:
- Before speaking, ask yourself: "Will this offend someone?"
- You are responsible for monitoring all behavior which can create a hostile or offensive environment for all employees.

MISTAKE 19 – *GIVE VAGUE EXPECTATIONS*

Once you and your employee have set goals as part of their annual performance review, it's easy to forget about them unless you've designed a system to track them as the year progresses. When you create a form, write out the goal, and consult the form during coaching sessions it is simple to trace results as the year goes on.

Many organizations have used SMART Goals in order to engage employees and foster accountability. SMART is an acronym for Specific, Measurable, Achievable, Results-oriented, and Timebound.

WRITE SMART GOALS

Written goals should specify what is to be done by when. Cost limitations should be included as appropriate. The statement should not include any reference to the means of accomplishing the objective.

Follow these guidelines:
- **Specific** – Say exactly what is to be achieved and to what extent. For example, to increase sales by 15%, to reduce absenteeism by 3 employee days per month, or to remodel the warehouse according to approved plans and budgets.
- **Measurable** – By being specific, the goal will be measurable. You will know whether you have been successful at the end of the performance period.
- **Achievable** – Goal statements should say what you are going to do. By being action-oriented and attainable they are more easily measured, and you will know whether or not you did as you intended.
- **Results-Oriented** – Good goal statements are realistic. They might be optimistic at the outset; but as the means to achieve them are developed, they should move into the realm of realism. Avoid extremes – such as 100% or 0 – that stand no chance of being accomplished.
- **Time bound** – Have a time limit built into them by which time the results will be achieved. People respond to deadlines. Without them things can easily be pushed farther into the future.

TIPS:
- Use documentation (reports, etc) to measure employee results.
- Receive a complimentary copy of the e-book, *Team Leadership Essentials: The Art of Risk & Motivation* by visiting www.78ManagerMistakes.com. Click on FREE RESOURCES tab and download *Art of Risk* ebook.

MISTAKE 20 – *MEETING MAYHEM*

Show of hands… how many of you enjoy going to meetings because they are productive? Not many, just as I thought. The problems with meetings seem endless – no agenda, too much in the agenda, out-of-control discussions, or no clear direction are just a few challenges.

As a manager, you will win over your team if you become efficient at planning the meeting, sticking to the agenda, rotating the meeting roles, and following up after the session. Here is a cheat sheet to create a successful meeting.

Before the Meeting:
1. Use an Agenda and include:
   - Purpose of the meeting and who needs to attend
   - Topics and who is leading that discussion item
   - Start/Stop times; Time allotted each topic
2. Assign the key meeting roles
   - Facilitator: Opens meeting, reviews agenda, focuses team on each topic, facilitates discussion, and manages participation.
   - Note-taker: Records main ideas, decisions made, and action items for each topic.
   - Timekeeper: Keeps track of posted times on the agenda.
3. Invite attendees stating the purpose of the meeting.

During the Meeting:
1. Start on time – don't penalize the team members that arrived when they should have.
2. Verify the facilitator, note taker, and timekeeper are on track.
3. Agree on any action items, deadlines, and person responsible for that item.

After the Meeting:
1. Review the meeting notes from the note-taker.
2. Distribute meeting notes within 24-hours of the meeting.

TIPS:
- Save yourself some time; determine if a meeting is really necessary.
- Try 5-Minute Stand-Up meetings throughout the day rather than a formal one hour session.

MISTAKE 21 – *AVOID CONFLICT*

Conflict is an inevitable part of any relationship. As you move from the "honeymoon" phase of building the team or, FORMING, you will enter into the STORMING phase. This is where true personalities come out and conflict intensifies.

The great news is there are volumes written on conflict resolution substantiated by years of research. You want to create an environment where both parties will have the opportunity to listen and offer their viewpoint.

Recommended Resources:
1. *Crucial Conversations, 2002,* (Patterson, Grenny, McMillan)
2. *QBQ! The Question Behind the Question, 2004,* (John G. Miller)
3. *How to Reduce Workplace Conflict and Stress, 2005,* (Anna Maravelas)
4. *The Coward's Guide to Conflict, 2003,* (Timothy Ursiny)

TIPS:
- Use the "I" Message technique to begin the conversation respectfully. It is a statement which describes the behavior, the effect that action has on you, the feelings you have about the action, and what the person can do to continue or modify the behavior.
- When you need to have a conversation between employees, be prepared. Do not "wing" it.

MISTAKE 22 – *UNABLE TO GIVE PRESENTATIONS*

You've worked hard to get to where you're at. You've gained experience and it shows. But does it show in all areas? Say, for example, when you need to give a presentation to the executive team?

Many people become tongue-tied when it comes to standing up in front of a group (large or small, it does not really matter). Your body also has a physical reaction – heart pounding, sweating, stomach queasiness, shortness of breath.

The big question is: How do you look cool, competent, and confident when giving the next presentation? You could ruin your stellar reputation with just one poorly executed talk.

Ways to Spoil a Speech:

1. **Wing it.** There are times you will need to make an impromptu speech, but always be well prepared for ones to which you received advance notice.
2. **Start out weak.** The audience may not remember all your key points, but they will remember how you made them feel when you started out.
3. **Make it all about you.** This is not the time or place to give a litany of your greatness. They came to hear how what you know will benefit them.
4. **Give only your opinion versus the facts.** Stick to the research. Draw conclusions and state your viewpoint, however, avoid bias and editorializing.
5. **Wander from your point.** Know your material well enough that you don't get side-tracked.
6. **Forget your objective.** What is the reason you were asked to speak? Always keep that objective in mind as you progress through the presentation. If in a meeting, track all ideas and suggestions not related to the topic and address them at another time.
7. **Finish weak.** Just as your audience remembers how you began, they will definitely remember how you concluded your presentation. Consciously plan the walk-away feeling and reiterate your main point.

TIPS:
- Prepare + Practice = Success
- For a cheat sheet of 27 techniques to help you prepare, deliver, and conclude a presentation, go to www.78ManagerMistakes.com. Download *Presentation Checklist* on the FREE RESOURCES tab.

MISTAKE 23 – *FORGET PROMISES*

As a manager, you are responsible for the results of your work group or department. You have probably been promoted to a lead position because of good work habits – keeping your word, meeting your deadlines, connecting with co-workers on both a personal and professional level.

One of the more advanced management skills necessary to competently perform your work is the ability to influence all members of your team to keep their commitments. How exactly do you get team members to be accountable for their own performance? How do you stay accountable with your boss?

At the very least, the agreement is a starting place for subsequent feedback and coaching sessions. At the very most, it's an effective method of keeping projects on target.

You have a Circle of Influence. The commitments you make to yourself and to others is the essence of your integrity and growth. You build the strength of character making promises, setting goals, and staying true to them.

You can make a promise and keep it. Or, you can set a goal and achieve it. As you make and keep commitments, you establish an inner integrity that gives you the awareness of self-control and the courage to accept more responsibility for your life. Little by little, keeping your promises increases your honor and employees find you more trustworthy.

The next time you're tempted to blow someone off consider this. There is a fellow employee or future co-worker on the other end of that commitment who was looking forward to interacting with you – to gain something from you, to share something with you, and maybe to learn from you.

TIPS:
- To avoid confusion over commitments, use a written agreement to identify goals, what actions you will take to meet the goal, the expected results, and the timeframe to complete the goal.
- Put your signature on the written agreement. There is a significant psychological factor involved in signing a document that clearly outlines your commitment and promise to complete it.

MISTAKE 24 – *HIRE ONLY FOR PERSONALITY*

Are you someone who 'goes with their gut' or someone who goes by the rules? When it comes to hiring employees, you need to find the balance between these two states. And, hire for the best job fit and culture fit from your pool of candidates.

Following the rules means you review and analyze the candidate's application, cover letter, portfolio, reference letters, and whatever else they submit.
When you look at job fit – job competencies – look at:
1. Measurable skills
2. Knowledge
3. Behavior
4. Interpersonal skills

However, it is only when a manager pays attention to a fifth category – attitude – that he or she can evaluate whether the candidate demonstrates a good cultural fit with the organization. This is where going with your instincts about the candidate comes into play.

Karen T, Zondervan Family Bookstore, Grand Rapids, MI shares her story:

"Shortly after starting as a new manager, I needed to hire a couple of people to take care of customers and run the cash register. The existing staff were good on the technical parts of the job, but I needed someone who was more personable.

I hired a woman who was friendly and bubbly, but ended up not being able to run the register very well. I made two mistakes. The first was being too trusting of the candidate without having any previous exposure to them. The second was being naïve in thinking that anyone can learn technical skills if they have a good personality and willingness to do so. Just because I learn quickly does not mean everyone can."

TIPS:
- Ask your Human Resources department for training on the legal aspects of hiring and terminating employees. You need to reduce liability to yourself and the organization.
- If possible, have multiple interviews with a candidate and have another person interview them as well. Another opinion is worth the effort.

MISTAKE 25 – *DODGE PERSONAL OPENNESS*

The age-old question is, How much personal information do you share with your staff and still be seen as their manager and a professional?

Maybe you've worked alongside these people for years, and moved from being a peer to their manager. If so, that doesn't mean you know them. It's even more important now, as their manager, to learn what makes them excited, how to motivate them, what they fear, what they worry about, and what rewards are meaningful to them.

Get to know your team members as individuals, because that is the only way you can effectively manage them. The relationship you have with your staff is what will make or break you in your pursuit to be a good manager.

On the flip side, just because you are the manager does not mean you can't be human. No one likes working with a robot so make it a point to laugh, show emotion, share your hobbies, show pictures of your family and pets, or make the occasional mistake.

TIPS:
- Connect more easily with team members by talking about your family, where you live, hobbies, travels, foods you enjoy, pets, music, sports, etc.
- Avoid controversial discussions that may be protected by law. Contact your Human Resources department if you are unsure and need to protect yourself and the company.

MISTAKE 26 – *DO IT ALL YOURSELF*

Sometimes, in an effort to be more likeable, managers want to become "friends" with their team. The downside to this approach is that it's easier for the employee to take advantage of your relationship.

Marsha Burger, Rocky Rocco's, Wauwatosa, WI shares her story:

"When I was promoted to manager in the restaurant, I continued to be "friends" with my staff. It led me to taking on all the responsibility of all work to be done. If they didn't do it (acting like they didn't have time to finish) I would do it. I ran myself ragged and they walked all over me.

I learned how to deploy work to others and helped them learn how and why they needed to take responsibility for their own work. By doing this, they also started taking more pride in what they were doing. I had a few employees come back to me after they had left the restaurant, and thank me for being so "hard" on them.

That gave me a feeling of complete satisfaction. It was a very painful, stressful and exhausting lesson to learn. I learned I could still breathe after giving up complete control of some things."

TIPS:
- Fully understanding the steps in delegation shifts workload where it belongs.
- Create a consistent practice of accountability for each team member's performance.

MISTAKE 27 – *FORGET EMAIL IS PUBLIC*

Communication – all forms – is a critical skill for every manager. The ability to clearly and concisely deliver your message in both verbal and written form determines how well you build relationships with your team, your boss, your customers.

Good communication takes time which seems contrary when using e-mail. E-mail is an informal method of communication; mostly jotting down thoughts. Without deliberate effort, it's easy to forget the feedback loop, not provide context, or follow-up with e-mail. In fact, 30-40% of miscommunication happens because of e-mail.

Business writing coach, Kit Behling, offers this key advice when writing and using e-mail:
1. Summarize the topic as precisely as you can (IE. New Client - Acme Inc.)
2. Provide a key piece of information (IE. Marketing project delayed to 3rd quarter)

Things that help…
- **Reply by or action date.** IE. Acme Claims Count: totals needed by xx/xx/xx or Performance Evaluations – new deadline xx/xx/xx
- **Action needed.** IE. Acme Final Report – proofreading needed
- **Benefit statement.** IE. New Reimbursement System: Get Travel Expenses Back Sooner

TIPS:
- When in doubt of your message, save it and sleep over it before hitting "Send.'"
- For longer memos, reports, or reference materials, share the information with team members using Google Docs or DropBox.com.
- Complimentary download of *Manager Email Checklist* at www.78ManagerMistakes.com, click on FREE RESOURCES tab.

MISTAKE 28 – *TAKE ACTION SLOWLY*

To be successful, you must take your ideas and implement them – **fast**. Don't hold back and do not dilly-dally with details and with trying to be perfect. Get your product or service out there and tweak as you go. Knowing that you and your team are taking something to the marketplace quickly, gives you a sense of movement.

I am not saying that you ignore good financial practices, skip research and development or survey customers on what they want. What I am saying is that not every idea, task or project needs to be over-analyzed. There is a difference between taking a calculated risk and being foolish. You want your team to be creative and try new things, and you do not want to waste precious company resources (people, time, money).

STRATEGIES FOR A SUCCESSFUL IMPLEMENTATION

- **Take immediate action.** Unsuccessful managers rarely ever implement anything they learn. They get caught in analysis paralysis.
- **Don't ask for everyone's opinion.** This is a waste of time especially if you are asking people who have not had success in this area.
- **Always be ready and willing to take action.** Have a clear plan for what you're trying to accomplish at all times.
- **The best time to take action is now.** The biggest reason you aren't able to do that is because you focus on information rather than the facts. Facts are based on undeniable truths and root causes. Information is based on thoughts and perceptions. Identify what you do know and what you don't know. Then, move on.

TIPS:
- Take at least one action **every day** that takes you closer to your goal. Switch your thinking from "projects and challenges" to "actions and outcomes." Focus on the ultimate outcome you want and the specific actions you must take to get it.
- Think about what success means to you and how you would get that. What is the one thing you could do right now? Take that action no matter how big or small and don't allow yourself to waiver from your decision.

MISTAKE 29 – *LACK CONFIDENCE*

One definition of confidence is: assurance; freedom from doubt; belief in yourself and your abilities. As a new manager, it will take a bit of work to understand true confidence in all your abilities versus the "fake it till you make it" kind. One thing that helps you to better develop confidence is a good understanding of your leadership style.

A true leadership style is one that is aligned with your values; not one where you have adapted to the organization's culture or to what your boss expects. If this finds you as a first-time manager, spend time figuring out who YOU are first.

THE 4 DIMENSIONS OF YOUR LEADERSHIP FOUNDATION

1. **Body – Connection to Nature.** The physical realm that is solid in the environment. How will you organize your work area? How will you care for your body through healthy eating and exercise?
2. **Mind – Connection to Beliefs.** The intellectual realm that has unshakable principles. What is your core philosophy about business and people? What values will you never compromise?
3. **Spirit – Connection to Others.** The inner self realm that impacts your relationship to those around you. What strengths do you bring to the team? Opportunities to get better? How do you show courage during tough times? What attitudes come out in your behavior? How are you received by others?
4. **Heart – Connection to Self.** The emotional realm that drives your thinking about yourself. How compassionate and empathetic are you with yourself? Others? What kindnesses do you show yourself and those around you? In what ways do you acknowledge your emotions, work through them, and use them appropriately in the workplace?

We all have different strengths and skills, and the workplace needs leaders who can use their voice to guide from a place of integrity. Find your voice!

TIPS:
- Take 15-minutes before you start the day to write out your answers to the questions posed in the 4 Dimensions of Your Leadership Foundation above. In only four days, you will have your foundation.
- Identify 1or 2 priorities in each of these areas that you will strengthen this year.

MISTAKE 30 – *PROCRASTINATION*

Old Definition of Procrastination:

"To put off intentionally and habitually; to delay"
(Merriam-Webster Dictionary)

Sad but true: On some level procrastination really works to motivate you. You will work fast and furious with a deadline looming on the horizon. The work, of course, will not be your best and you will most likely feel the urge to point that out to anyone who will listen. Circumstances may have come together so you had no other options than to delay. I have a feeling; however, the real story is you made a series of choices to put yourself into a procrastination mode.

TOP 3 WARNING SIGNS OF PROCRASTINATION

1. **Fear of** – making a mistake, failing, being blamed for negative results.
2. **Intense Feelings** – powerless, frustrated, depressed, pressured, stressed.
3. **Skewed Sense About Time** – lose track of time when working on a project, always late for meetings, you are often heard to say, "That project will be finished sometime next week."

While these warning signs can appear for everyone, as a manager, you may also notice your team feeling like victims, being overwhelmed, and afraid of being criticized.

The best thing you can do is to stop judging yourself (or those on your team) as lazy, and realize that procrastination is just a coping method. It is in uncovering and eliminating the underlying fear that you will end the procrastination cycle.

New Definition of Procrastination:
"An attempt – albeit an unsatisfactory one – at coping with the often incapacitating fear of having our worth held up for judgment."
(Dr. Neil Fiore)

TIPS:
- Look for ways to cultivate commitment from your staff and yourself.
- Liberally give constructive encouragement. As Ken Blanchard says, "Catch people doing things RIGHT."
- Know your team priorities. Keep goals clear so there isn't the opportunity to consider procrastinating.

MISTAKE 31 – *DON'T PROTECT YOUR TEAM*

Everyone is under pressure. It comes at you from all directions:

- Other departments may want to blame you for failed interactions.
- Your boss may want to dump all the unpleasant jobs on your department.
- The CFO may decide all job classifications in your area are overpaid.
- Your customer may be screaming that your best team member caused a $10,000 error.

In your position as manager, it is your job to be the buffer between your team and the outside forces against them. Assertiveness, or "standing up for yourself," is a valuable skill to have. It is the difference between responding actively to the situation or person versus passively taking what someone is throwing at you.

HOW TO BE MORE ASSERTIVE

1. Stand up straight and breathe.
2. Look the other person in the eye.
3. Remember you have a right to be heard. Your opinions and needs need to be considered when decisions are being made.
4. Be direct and specific. Deliver your message in short, easy-to-understand sentences, respectfully offering or asking for clarification if needed.
5. Be prepared and practice. If there is someone you need to confront, take the time to prepare the message you wish to get across. Practice saying the message while paying close attention to your tone of voice and body language.

Being assertive does not mean being arrogant. Your goal is to keep the lines of communication, compromise, and negotiation open.

TIPS:
- Stand up for each person on your team and make sure they are treated as fairly as possible.
- Keeping good documentation on projects will verify the contribution of team members.

MISTAKE 32 – *IGNORE PERSONAL LOSS*

Your management journey starts by looking inward to understand WHY you are here and WHAT it is that you are here to do. Before you can manage others, you have to discover yourself. You cannot impose yourself on others; you make yourself available to others.

It is in the knowing of yourself that you have the ability to help a team member who is suffering. Most organizations have clearly defined funeral/bereavement leave for any death, sometimes even non-family members. Yet, grief does not heal within the typical 3-day leave.
What else can you as a manager do to support a team member going through the grief cycle? *Consider:*
- Temporary reduction in workload.
- Providing a good listening ear. Sincerely ask how they are doing.
- Offering to transfer employee closer to family (if possible).
- Giving a book on grieving.
- Collecting cash to help offset unexpected funeral expenses.
- Making phone calls to "just check in."
- Providing additional time off if they are having an especially bad day trying to cope with grief.
- Doing something concrete rather than just making an offer to help.
- Allowing them to take Sick Leave (rather than Bereavement Leave) if your company has a strict interpretation of the word "family." These days, many folks have been raised by aunts and uncles rather than biological parents.

Remember, grieving is a long process. Employees who are allowed to fully grieve are more likely to return to work sooner and concentrate better than those who lack support.

TIPS:
- When you see a grieving employee struggling at work, be a good listener who does not pass judgment or make gratuitous suggestions.
- Do not pretend everything is fine and nothing happened.

MISTAKE 33 – *GIVE ORDERS*

There was a time when being a good manager was defined as giving orders to the people below you. Granted, that thinking was prevalent decades ago, however, you see evidence of it again in the workplace today. The distinction between "giving orders" and "giving instructions."

Giving orders is:
- Telling someone to do something.
- Not allowing the person any latitude to think about what to do or how to do it.
- Only accepting satisfactory performance if the order is carried out **exactly**.

Why are giving orders bad? First, you hinder the person from figuring out the best way to complete the task. Second, you stifle their learning.

Giving instructions include:
- Telling an employee **what** you want done.
- Allowing the employee freedom to come up with the best way of doing a task.
- Monitoring the task and offering needed guidance.
- Encouraging the employee to think versus blindly doing as they are told.
- Allowing the employee to invest themselves in the solution.

Why is giving instructions better? By letting the employee decide on a course of action, you will more likely get their buy-in and support. If they made the decision, then they will believe it is correct and valuable. They will also defend it against those who question it.

TIPS:
- Allow the team to get things done that do not limit their level of expertise.
- Let everyone contribute whatever they can, even if it is not accomplished exactly how you would complete it. Your goal is to nurture team creativity and involvement.

MISTAKE 34 – *SHOW FAVORITISM*

Like it or not, favoritism is part of human nature. Favoritism at work refers to when someone appears to be treated better than another based on perceived preferential treatment and not superior work performance. In other words, you give special privileges to someone because of who they know rather than on their ability to do the job.

It is perfectly acceptable to interact more with an employee who is doing excellent work, and you have given them added responsibility. It makes sense that there would be more interaction between you.

Favoritism becomes an issue, however, when you actually provide unfair preferential treatment for one employee at the expense of others. *Nepotism* is the ultimate workplace favoritism. In both these cases, you stand the chance of violating the rights of other employees qualified to take on additional assignments.

Scenarios of potential favoritism might include:
- Being promoted faster than others unfairly.
- Being paid more to do the same job as others.
- Being given more flexibility to come and go during the day.

TIPS:
- Know your company's human resources policies on the issue. Keep yourself and your employer safe from legal action.
- Track the favors you are giving among your team members. Ask yourself: Am I more lenient with just a few people? Am I basing my decision to grant a special request equally among everyone?

MISTAKE 35 – *TALK DOWN TO PEOPLE*

In the workplace, you do not have to be more powerful than the people you are being condescending to. Talking down to people – being condescending – is really quite simple. All you need to do is elevate yourself while putting down others.

There is healthy conflict, but conflict becomes destructive when condescending conversational tones are used. For some managers, it is an automatic conversational technique, and for others it is an aggressive intention. Regardless, condescension hurts everyone involved.

Have you been told that you talk down to people? Realize that there are three different patterns that require three different approaches to overcome.

1. **Habitual** – sometimes a habit, a cultural difference, or a cultural preference.
2. **Reciprocal** – a mirrored response to someone else who started speaking in a condescending tone first
3. **Intentional** – a deliberate tactic often used to be intimidating, issue an insult, or create superiority in your own mind

Examples of condescending statements include:
- We already thought of that.
- Let me see if I can put this in terms simple enough for you.
- Well, I'm glad you could finally join us.
- Oh, you just figured that out?

TIPS:
- Pay attention to condescending remarks by counting how often they are used in your workplace. Note any trends. Is it the same person? On the same topic? Ask yourself: Am I also talking down to others?
- If you are talking down to people, make a conscious decision to stop. It is your decision. What other ways can you resolve the issue rather than resorting to using a technique that can easily escalate negative emotions? It's your choice.

MISTAKE 36 – *DON'T NETWORK ENOUGH*

Marla Holman, Training Director, Western States Envelope & Label, Butler, WI relates her story:

"I started at Western States Envelope in Production and, over time, was promoted to Training Director. I adopted the organizations' leadership and management style, and became very focused on a heavy workload. There was little time left over to become involved in networking.

But guess what? When my job was eliminated, the companies out there have some very different styles. It would have helped me now if I had been more participative in meeting and talking with peers in other companies.

Not only would I have been aware of other company cultures, and better prepared for a job hunt, but I could have added value to my employer by sharing "best practices" from the organizations I was networking with."

TIPS:
- Become involved with one external organization where you can increase your professional development. Go beyond just attending an occasional meeting. Enhance your association by attending regularly and participating during any open networking time. Consider volunteering on a committee.
- If you really are strapped for time, join an online forum of managers within your industry and participate in the discussions.

MISTAKE 37 – *FORGET REWARDS*

Turn on any nightly newscast and you will hear doom-and-gloom economic predictions. One of the first places you will be asked to curtail expenses often affects the very people who keep your business going… Your Staff.

Managers who can balance the bottom-line without sacrificing the spirit of the team are managers who will weather economic highs and lows effectively. Your team members are doing their job and performing well, and it's only human nature for them to want acknowledgment for those efforts.

10 NO-COST RECOGNITION IDEAS

- **Use praise.** You know this one yet many managers find it hard to do in-the-moment.
- **Increase team member visibility.** Send a group email, let your CEO know, or announce it during a staff meeting.
- **Give information.** Employees crave accurate information so communicate often and early.
- **Increase team member involvement.** Create ways to solicit individual opinions on issues facing your organization.
- **Offer interesting work.** Create opportunities for the individual to work on a special project team.
- **Give feedback on performance.** Report back more frequently what you see being accomplished.
- **Listen, Really Listen!** Consciously practice deeper listening to understand and connect with the individual.
- **Allow flexibility.** If it is not critical to customers, can you allow the individual freedom in establishing their work hours and time off?
- **Recommend independence.** Offer in-house training that allows the individual to learn a new skill.
- **Play.** As adults, we are not often allowed to "play" at work yet it relieves stress and improves morale. Consider lunchtime walks, team stretch breaks, Joke of the Day challenge, or Silly Socks Day.

TIPS:
- Create an ongoing department Reward and Recognition Program. The key is consistency over time rather than a one-time event.
- Low-cost rewards can be found at: www.baudville.com or www.successories.com

MISTAKE 38 – *DON'T DEAL WITH OUTBURSTS*

Let me acquaint you with the term "emotional intelligence."

Daniel Goleman in his books *Emotional Intelligence* (Bantam, 1995) and *Primal Leadership* (HBS Press, 2002) describes emotions as "an evolved signal system and emotional intelligence (EI) as the process of learning to be aware of and to regulate one's emotions." He goes on to say that EI "accounts for as much as 70% of individual performance while cognitive ability and technical learning account for only 30%."

EI is more than "warm and fuzzy" because it can unlock productivity and creativity in a way that nothing else does.

THE MANAGER'S ROLE

Moving individual emotional intelligence to a group norm gets introduced through multiple ways. What can you as the leader do to work with these three dimensions (individual level, group level, cross-boundary level)?

Your key responsibility here is to help create an environment that encourages team members to deepen their commitment to the team. Encourage them to:
- Speak out whenever they disagree with a team goal issue.
- Speak up for those who are not present.

3 WAYS TO GROW YOUR TEAM'S EMOTIONAL INTELLIGENCE

1. Develop the Team's emotional vocabulary.
2. Practice empathy and empathetic communication.
3. Learn to speak up and to listen.

Rule of thumb: Teams with high customer contact require highly developed emotional skills. Those that focus on technical skills (for example, finance and IT teams) do not.

TIPS:
- Consider using assessments in understanding the emotions and group dynamics of your staff. Top picks: ECI-360, EQ-i, MSCEIT
- Figuring out the EI of you and your team helps to resolve conflict.

MISTAKE 39 – *IGNORE THE UNWRITTEN RULES*

Understand that no matter how similar the culture seems to others you've experienced, your new organization is going to have its own unique quirks. "Learn how things get done — both the rational and irrational aspects of it," advises Nat Stoddard, chairman of Crenshaw Associates.

Often referred to as a game, office politics does play a role in who succeeds faster within an organization than others. Whether you are highly skilled at the game, disinterested in playing, or frustrated that mediocre talent has been promoted faster than you does not matter. What does matter is that you can choose your involvement based on a better understanding of the subtleties of office politics.

How to win at office politics sounds so, well, cut-throat. What I'm proposing is developing a sense of genuine self, and living in a corporate environment the way you want to live those hours of your life.

Habits are patterns of behavior you can incorporate into daily practice. Change begins with a thought that something can be different. You can look at these habits as a way to view office politics in a more favorable light. More importantly, they offer a new routine to live more sincerely through the negativity of the office political scene.

1. It is your choice whether or not to participate in office politics.
2. Know your goals and organizational goals. Always focus on the business objectives. Do not take sides between feuding parties. Do not get personal.
3. Focus on your circle of influence; the things that you can do to influence the situation.
4. Seek to understand, before being understood. This is courtesy of Stephen Covey's work in *The 7 Habits of Highly Effective People*. Instinctively, we are more interested in getting others to understand us rather than to understand them first. Learn to suppress the urge to defend your position first.

TIPS:
- Listen carefully when colleagues give you tips on the best time of day to approach a senior manager.
- Pay attention to the stories told about happenings within the office. Just don't seem overly curious.

MISTAKE 40 – *BECOME EXCLUSIVE TOO QUICKLY*

There are some subtle differences between networking in general and networking within your own organization. In either case, your aim is to build long-lasting, genuine relationships.

The art of networking looks effortless when we observe someone in, say, the Sales and Marketing Department. But, you may be thinking it's too hard for you or your position doesn't require interaction with many others in the company. You would be limiting yourself with both those thoughts.

If you are serious about getting known in your organization and making a contribution, here is an easy activity to do as you begin working on your internal network.

Who Do You Already Know?
Grab a sheet of paper and quickly list 2-3 people you know today in each of the following departments:

Accounting	Human Resources	Marketing/PR	Quality
Customer Service	Inform. Systems	Medical/Wellness	Reception
Executive Level	Mail Room	Product Develop.	Sales
Facilities	Maintenance	Purchasing	Security

Look at the names on your list and think back to how you were introduced. Did you find them on your own or were you introduced through someone else?

Being new, your goal is to connect with a broad spectrum of folks in your organization; not stick with a clique. You can easily spot the gaps in your internal network by department. This gives you the opportunity of prioritizing which connections to develop first. Remember:

"People will do business with people they know, like, and trust." – Unknown

TIPS:
- Carve out 2 lunches per week to connect with someone you don't know in another department.
- Maintain ongoing relationships by having coffee with those people twice weekly on a rotating basis.

MISTAKE 41 – *DON'T UNDERSTAND TEAM ROLES/RESPONSIBILITIES*

Let's start off by clarifying terminology around two areas:
1. What positions are necessary on a team (Roles)
2. What tasks those positions need to carry out (Responsibilities)

There are many good team building resources for a manager in today's work environment. This simple guide takes the complexity out of understanding a team structure.

Team Roles
Four basic team roles exist: Team Sponsor, Team Member, Team Leader, Team Coach.

TEAM SPONSOR – A higher "ranking" employee (usually a Department Manager or Vice President) who identifies improvement projects, has authority to allot resources to the team, reviews results, and takes team recommendations further into the organization.

TEAM MEMBER – Anyone who contributes their knowledge, skills, and abilities to the work of the team. In essence, everyone assigned to a team is considered a team member.

TEAM LEADER – The person who serves as the link between team members and the rest of the organization by coordinating team activities and maintaining all team documentation.

TEAM COACH – An individual experienced in team building skills, communication, resolving problems, and analyzing data. This person helps any team member.

Team Responsibilities
For ease, the chart below outlines only the major tasks of each team role.

ROLE RESPONSIBILITY

Role	Responsibility
TEAM SPONSOR	• Maintains overall authority and accountability • Selects improvement project and drafts team charter • Establishes resources • Selects all team role assignments and evaluates their progress • Monitors implementation changes for improvement project
TEAM MEMBER	• Participates fully in all meetings to share their knowledge • Communicates completely by listening without assumptions • Completes all assigned tasks
TEAM LEADER	• Establishes and sustains ways for team members to complete their tasks • Uses multiple problem-solving methods; data analysis • Creates communication channels between team, Sponsor, and all other organization departments • Updates Sponsor on project progress • Has management authority to implement recommended changes
TEAM COACH	• Uses interpersonal communication skills effectively (how to build a team, giving and receiving feedback, conflict resolution) • Maintains technical aspects (project management, root cause methodology, planning) • Serves as team trainer for both interpersonal and technical information

TIPS:
- When shifting to a team-based structure, educate every team member on each of the new roles and responsibilities.
- Do not use this structure if you cannot consistently maintain it.

MISTAKE 42 – *SLOPPY DECISION-MAKING*

Decision: A determination arrived at after consideration; a report of a conclusion; promptness and firmness in deciding; determination.
(Merriam-Webster Dictionary)

Teams need to discuss what is important and the method / process for reporting conclusions in order to make wise decisions for their organization. Here are the key components to make better decisions.

1. **Be Clear You Understand the Context of the Decision.**
    - Clarify the decision. Does everyone know exactly what is being decided?
    - Know the deadlines. Does everyone understand the consequences if a decision is not made?
    - Collect relevant data. Does everyone comprehend how past and pending decisions relate to each other?

2. **Decide Who Needs to Be Involved in the Decision. ASK:**
    - Who has the authority to make the decision?
    - Who is ultimately responsible for the results?
    - Who will be affected by the decision immediately and in the future?
    - Who has critical information we need to make the decision?

3. **Choose a Decision-Making Method.**
   There are multiple methods for making a decision such as a team vote, one person decides (best used in an emergency situation), or by a subgroup of the team (such as experts). Each of these methods has strengths and weaknesses, but I will focus on the one method most often used by teams… CONSENSUS.

What is Consensus?
- Everyone understands the decision and can explain why it is best.
- Everyone can live with the decision.
- Everyone discussed the issue and took all sides into consideration.
- Everyone expressed their current viewpoint and answered questions posed by the team.

What is NOT Consensus?
- Everyone getting what they want.
- Everyone agreeing to a compromise.
- Everyone agreeing to a unanimous vote.

Consensus Works Best When…
- Decisions are important and affect many people.
- The team has 10 or fewer members.
- The team has lots of ideas to exchange, whether in person, by phone, or video conferencing.

TOP TIPS FOR SUCCESSFUL CONSENSUS

1. **Listen carefully.** Be open and watch your assumptions about what is being said. Ask for the speaker's reasons if you are unclear.
2. **Encourage all team members to contribute.** Silence does not necessarily mean the person agrees. Go around the circle and have each team member state their viewpoint.
3. **Diligently search for options that meet the goals of the team.** Do not think in terms of "winning" or "losing." When there is a disagreement, look for the next best alternative for everyone.
4. **Do not change your mind only to avoid conflict.**
5. **Do not argue only for your position.** Can your idea be combined with someone else's?
6. **Allow enough time to come to consensus.** Here is the down-side to consensus…it takes time. Since everyone is expressing their opinion and everyone on the team needs to agree with the decision, the meeting should be long enough to give each person the opportunity to speak and ask clarifying questions.

TIPS:
- Do not ask for team input if you have already made a decision. It is disrespectful and a waste of time.
- Schedule enough time if you are making a decision by team consensus. The up-side of this method is the high degree of trust and understanding you create.

MISTAKE 43 – *FEAR OVERLOAD*

It is natural to have some trepidation when starting a new position; more so when you're the manager. The level of responsibility for your staff, customers, and organization are enormous.

My first promotion to Training Director caused 3-months of nightmares. Why? Because I, wrongly, focused on all the negative self-talk. I was operating from the "What if" and "What will I do" modes of self-doubt. It became so overwhelming that fear perpetuated itself.

Susan Jeffers in her book, *Feel the Fear and Do It Anyway*, says, "Pushing through fear is less frightening than living with the underlying fear that comes from a feeling of helplessness." She also offers seven ways to reclaim your power.

It is in the reclaiming of your power that your "self" comes through. When your confidence is enhanced you begin to believe that you can achieve your goals rather than just "hoping" they will be completed. There are some things you have no outside control over. Look at these 3 levels of fears:

Level 1 – The Surface Story. These consist of thing that happen to you (such as aging, retirement, being alone, natural disasters, change, war, illness, accidents) and things that require action (think – going back to school, changing a career, making friends, asserting yourself, losing weight, being interviewed, public speaking, making a mistake).

Level 2 – Inner states of mind (Ego). Rejection, success, failure, being vulnerable, helplessness, disapproval, loss of image to name a few.

Level 3 – The Biggest Fear of All. "I can't handle it!"

The truth is: If you knew you could handle anything that came your way, what would you possibly have to fear? Answer: Nothing!

TIPS:
- Read Susan Jeffers book, *Feel the Fear and Do It Anyway*. Integrate her No-Lose Decision method (page 113) into your management techniques.
- Remember, acknowledgment of fear is very important; denial is deadly.

MISTAKE 44 – *IGNORE PROFESSIONAL DEVELOPMENT*

Yes, you just were promoted to manager but this is also the best time to think beyond your new position. Do you have a sense of where you want to be in your career 5-10 years from now? What about just 2 years from now? Maybe, but right now you are more focused on what education and training you need to do the current job.

WAYS TO INCREASE CURRENT SKILLS AND KNOWLEDGE

1. Join **and regularly attend** your industry's association meetings.
2. Start a Peer Focus Group with the express purpose of learning from each other. Have a Topic-of-the-Month.
3. Complete your Bachelor's or Master's degree.
4. Find industry or job-specific discussion groups on LinkedIn.
5. Subscribe to your industry magazine. Read it!
6. Subscribe to online e-newsletters geared to your position.

Organizations thrive on having strong leadership in place, and you have the possibility of entering their succession planning process based on the work you are performing now. Succession planning allows a company to identify their emerging leaders. In essence, it is a process where an organization ensures that employees are recruited and developed to fill each key role within the company. You want to be on that list.

Do your goals include moving into a senior management role? If so, that role will require several different competencies than your current management role requires. *Competencies such as:*

- Commitment and courage
- Communication and clarity
- Character and compassion

TIPS:
- Include at least one professional development goal in your annual review.
- Further your development with a customized Team Fusion WORKSHOP or TEAMBUILDING EVENT (more information on page 100).

MISTAKE 45 –*UNGRATEFULNESS*

Some new managers find themselves in a Catch-22 position: 1) in need of lots of help in beginning their job and 2) fear of appearing incompetent because they need help. Do you find that it's easier to help others but not accept help from others? Why do you say "No" when people offer to help you? Why do you refuse generosity from others?

There are many possible reasons you may struggle with asking for and/or accepting help. Some likely rationale includes:
1. You do not believe you are worthy of help and generosity. Accepting help from others is a form of taking care of yourself. By allowing others to lend a hand, you are sending a message to yourself that you deserve assistance.
2. You do not want to inconvenience others. Most people do not offer help unless they are sincere and are in a position to do so. While accepting offered help is hard, because you might have a fear that you are putting someone out, asking for help may be even more difficult. If you have a balanced and humble approach to asking for help, then there is nothing to feel guilty about.
3. You think you can do it better than anyone else. You've heard the saying, "If you want something done right, you better do it yourself." If you are a person who lives by this motto, you may find yourself juggling too many things because you need a sense of control. And, control is something difficult for most managers to release.

As a manager you do not always need to be strong. Give your team the opportunity to serve you from time to time. They will surprise you, and you will be given a breather to regroup when you may need it most.

TIPS:
- Ask for help a few times per week, with the intention that you are doing it to grow.
- Accept help a few times per week, reminding yourself that you do not need to control every aspect of a task.

MISTAKE 46 – *ALLOW NEGATIVITY*

An aspect of dealing with difficult people is that it may not be with just one person. What happens if the behavior is pervasive within the team itself? I recommend the following:

HOW TO TAKE NEGATIVITY OUT OF TEAMS

1. Establish clear roles and responsibilities.
2. Set clear ground rules.
   - Put one person in charge of enforcing the ground rules.
   - Establish a consequence for those who break the rules.
3. Bring structure to team activities.

Finally, even in the best circumstances there may come a time where you simply cannot "take" anymore. The following techniques for appearing calm and in control – even when you are not – will help increase your credibility as a manager:

- Take several deep breaths.
- Use positive self-talk to prepare mentally for the next conversation.
- Take a drink of water.
- Change positions.
- Take a break and deal with the situation later. Specify exactly when you will deal with it.

The key is to remain calm and deal with the other person in a respectful manner while maintaining your leadership role.

TIPS:
- Watch for a trend toward negativity. If there is one, address the situation quickly.
- Do not participate in a conversation that bashes another person's character.

MISTAKE 47 – *HIDE IN YOUR OFFICE*

You have finally made it and advanced to a manager title. Years of hard work have paid off and now you can sit back and enjoy the perks of your new position. Hardly!

Yes, you will be spending more time tucked away in your office to tackle:
1. More administrative work – writing reports, approving requests, responding to customer inquiries.
2. Confidential situations – writing performance reviews, holding interviews, coaching employees.
3. Special projects – those assigned by your boss.

Your goal, however, is to gain the trust and respect of your team which does not happen with a closed door policy. When staff constantly sees you ignoring them, they will begin to resent the distance you are creating.

You learn more about individual personalities and customer needs by walking the floor and interacting with your team. Additionally, it allows you the opportunity to see for yourself how team members are treating each other. It is the perfect time to catch them doing things right, and recognizing that during a formal coaching session.

TIPS:
- Do not close your door for 8-hours a day. If you need the privacy to work on projects, post your Office Hours so the team knows when you are available.
- Carry a small notepad – or 3x5 cards – when walking through your department. Jot down the request so you can quickly get an answer to that employee.

MISTAKE 48 – *CONSTANTLY PUT OUT FIRES*

You will encounter unforeseen "bumps" in the road. But there is a big difference in dealing with the occasional "bump" and working each day only in the "putting out fires" mode.

Being new to your position, is a great time to look at the department's contingency plans for when things go wrong. It allows you to tap into the knowledge level of your team, and learn the processes they use in getting their job done. If you need to create contingency plans because none exist.

In *Making Things Happen: Mastering Project Management*, Scott Berkun, a former program manager for Microsoft's biggest projects, offers advice for dealing with unexpected catastrophes. Here's a condensed version of his steps to get a project back on track:

1. Calm down. Nothing makes a situation worse than basing your actions on fear, anger, or frustration.
2. Evaluate the problem in relation to the project. Just because someone else thinks the sky has fallen doesn't mean that it has. Put things in perspective and then prioritize when you will act: emergency (now!), big concern (today), minor concern (this or next week), or bogus (never).
3. Get the right people in the room. Any major problem won't affect you alone. Identify who else is most responsible, knowledgeable, and useful, and get them together right away. Keep this group small. Offer your support, but get out of their way (leave the room if you're not needed). Do not let the meeting break up without identifying who will drive the resolution.
4. Explore alternatives. After answering any questions and clarifying the situation, list your options.
5. Make the simplest plan. Weigh the options and pick the best choice.
6. Execute. Make it happen — and make sure whoever drives the action plan has an intimate understanding of why he is doing it.
7. Debrief. After the fire is out, get the right people in the room again and generate a list of lessons learned.

TIPS:
- Use a staff meeting to decide what contingency plans need to be written.
- Designate a sub-team to write the initial plans before getting input from the larger team.

MISTAKE 49 – PLAY POLITICS

It would be best if your boss or co-workers would never have the chance to "get" you. Many times bad behavior toward you has nothing to do with you personally. The workplace setting brings out the worst in people; especially during economic slow-downs. Human nature will do everything to deflect negativity and turn it toward someone else.

But, participating in proactive politics is a way of navigating the political waters positively. Ward off gossip and backstabbing in the first place by:

- Asking respected managers for guidance – If your organization has a mentoring program, take advantage of it early in your tenure. This will be the person you can go to figure out the way business decisions are made and who has influence.
- Be strategic in offering help – Spread goodwill in your department by staying late to help a team member meet a deadline. Go out of your way to sincerely thank someone for any kindness they have shown toward you.
- Create visibility with important projects – Let everyone know exactly what work you completed. It can be as simple as emailing key stakeholders a short project summary and asking for input. You want to avoid having someone else take the credit for your efforts.

TIPS:
- Build a relationship with someone well-liked and well-thought of in the company. Periodically ask for their advice. They are more likely to defend you when you need it most if you are not an unknown employee.
- If you suspect someone of sabotaging your career, ask yourself: Am I being left out of the loop? Are resources being taken away? Who is behind this?
- Receive a complimentary copy of the e-book, *Team Leadership Essentials: The Art of Office Politics* by visiting www.78ManagerMistakes.com. Click on FREE RESOURCES tab and download *Office Politics* ebook.

MISTAKE 50 – *UNDER-DEVELOP THE WHOLE TEAM*

You want people on your team that you can count on. The caution here is to develop the skill set of every team member rather than relying on just a couple of people. Having "go to" people is nice because you begin to communicate in shorthand over time.

The downside, however, is that your work could potentially have missing perspectives that affect the quality and overall performance. Plus, your own performance is being measured by the efforts of your whole team.

Drafting a **Team Charter** will help focus attention, develop a timeline with priorities, define success, and develop all members in the work group.

An effective charter will help a team:
1. Understand the problem.
2. Define the importance of the problem to the organization (employees and customers).
3. Determine the scope of the project.
4. Outline the key deliverables and how success will be measured.
5. Identify principal project team members and time allocation.

TIPS:
- Invite all team members to participate in the creation of a Team Charter. They will, after all, be the ones living by it.
- Need guidance writing a team charter? Download the *Team Charter* form on the FREE RESOURCES tab at www.78ManagerMistakes.com.

MISTAKE 51 – *FORGET TO MANAGE UPWARDS*

Boss management can stimulate better performance, improve your working life, increase job satisfaction, and balance workload. Jacques Horovitz Professor of Service Strategy at IMD, interviewed 250 managers about managing their boss. His aim was to help the manager/direct report relationship become more effective, foster faster decisions, and build trust.

Here are his results (Rediff News, August 12, 2005):

1. *Decisions:* If you do not want a "no" or procrastination, give him/her a hand.
2. *Manage their time:* See Mistake #7.
3. *An opinion:* If you ask for an opinion, he/she will always have one.
4. *Information:* It is not data.
5. *Problems:* Do not just come with problems, come also with solutions.
6. *Assumptions:* Do not assume your boss knows as much as you do, but assume he/she can understand; so educate. " Please help. You are the expert." You live with the data; your boss does not.
7. *Delegations:* Constantly test the waters.
8. *Promises:* Do not promise what you cannot deliver, and avoid surprises, trust is at stake.
9. *Differences:* Manage differences in culture.
10. *Trust:* Do not be sloppy in your documentation. It undermines trust.

TIPS:
- Tell your boss what you expect from him/her; simply to inform, to decide jointly, to share the risk, to re-examine the option, etc.
- Make sure your boss does not get the information from others too often. Do not be shy if you know something that is relevant. It avoids your boss saying, "Why didn't you tell me that?"
- Receive your complimentary copy of the e-book, *Team Leadership Essentials: The Art of Managing Your Boss* by visiting www.78ManagerMistakes.com. Click on FREE RESOURCES tab and download *Managing Your Boss*. This book gives you more in-depth information on how to nurture your most important relationship.

MISTAKE 52 – *CREATE A DEMOTIVATING ENVIRONMENT*

Tap into the two forms of employee motivation – intrinsic and extrinsic – which help prevent creating a workplace where employees do not want to do their best work.

Intrinsic Employee Motivation – This form of motivation you have within yourself that comes from a passion or interest in doing a job well done.

Extrinsic Employee Motivation – This form of motivation is external and relies on recognition and rewards.

The challenge is in designing a comprehensive program incorporating both the intrinsic and extrinsic motivation needs of employees. Take the time to include both forms and watch your team performance grow far beyond previous levels.

BENEFITS OF HIGH EMPLOYEE MOTIVATION

- Creates a workplace and culture of high achievers
- Improves business and workforce productivity
- Reduces employee turnover
- Decreases in absenteeism and sick days

3 WAYS TO JUMPSTART INTRINSIC EMPLOYEE MOTIVATION

1. Purpose – Create a culture with a strong mission statement.
2. Belief – Help employees believe in what your company sells.
3. Passion – Hire the person who has passion for that job.

3 WAYS TO JUMPSTART EXTRINSIC EMPLOYEE MOTIVATION

1. Rewards – Personalize the reward to the recipient.
2. Recognition – Make recognition timely.
3. Growth – Put employee development at the top of your list.

TIPS:
- Introduce new employees to the team and use ice-breakers at staff meetings to help the group know each other better.
- Provide opportunities for employees to expand their knowledge.

MISTAKE 53 – *THINK YOUR IMAGE DOESN'T MATTER*

Whether you like it or not, everything about you, from appearance to your way of thinking, sends a message to others. People make assumptions and judgments about your abilities based on their perception of you in various situations. How do you interact with co-workers? Your management staff? Your suppliers?

Much like large corporations, you can create your own personal brand. It's simply what people think when they hear your name or see you in action rather than what they think when they hear your company's name.

- Dedicate time to make it happen. In other words, create and implement a master plan surrounding you.
- Do everything with a creative flair. Memorability is a vital link to building awareness.
- Stay in front of the people you want to do business with both internal and external. It takes between 5 – 10 images to create awareness big enough to make you "top of mind".
- Become a resource. It is more powerful than being perceived as a salesman; just building a connection to get something. People will want to be around you, and pay attention to what you say; if they believe what you say and do has value to them and their goals.
- Have a good time networking. People who take it too seriously have problems sorting out what is important in the world.
- Become known as a person of action.
- Update your wardrobe, if necessary. Dress appropriately for the organizational level to which you want to connect.

It only takes 3 seconds to make an impression!

A. **Appearance**
   - Style of dress; clothes fit well and in good repair
   - Personal grooming (hair, make-up, fragrance)
   - Your office décor
   - The cleanliness of your vehicle

B. **Networking Etiquette**
   - WIIFM (What's in it for me?) Put yourself into your potential connections place. What is the benefit to them of knowing you?
   - MMFI-AM (Make me feel important – About me) How can you make the other person feel good and be of help to them?

C. Making Introductions
- Introduce others by deferring to position and age. For example, introduce younger to older; fellow executive to client; personal contact to business contact.
- Make a brief statement and mention something both have in common.

D. Telephone and E-mail Etiquette
- Give specific subject line in emails.
- Turn on vacation notice when you're out of the office.
- Re-read your email before clicking Send.
- Leave a meaningful phone message
(purpose of call, how much time you will need, who referred you, etc).
- Answer within 24-hours.

TIPS:
- Determine the one characteristic about you that you want to be known for. Incorporate that into your branding. Can it translate into your clothing, office, management style, decision-making, etc?
- Spend some time thinking about: What one thing can I do consistently (without going broke) that makes me memorable to co-workers and clients alike? Some examples: handwritten Thank You cards, always using a signature color ink pen, a lapel pin, the same phrase at the end of a voicemail message.

MISTAKE 54 – *BURNOUT*

At all costs, you want to keep yourself and the team from job burnout.
How do you know if someone who reports to you is suffering from burnout?

WARNING SIGNS:

1. Chronic fatigue
2. Anger; exploding easily
3. Self-criticism for putting up with demands
4. Cynicism
5. Negativity
6. Irritability
7. Sleeplessness
8. Weight loss or gain
9. Suspiciousness

Having the "blues" is often described as a sense of melancholy – this could be being down in the dumps, low, glum unhappy, or despondent. How do you avoid this emotional state when you have work overload, problem jobs, deal with problem people, or the work environment is filled with tension?

A. **Create a Defense Shield** – Set yourself up for success first. Put another way, build a system of self-care that gives you work/life balance.
B. **Evaluate and Manage Your Job Performance** – Eliminate unnecessary worry about the quality of your work and how you are doing. A simple question to ask yourself: Do I have an annual performance plan and am I following it?
C. **Apply Relaxation Techniques** – Organizations are beginning to understand the value of wellness programs and the positive affect they have on team members who participate. Take advantage of an activity you find fun and enjoy doing.

TIPS:
- Create a space in which employees can do their best work.
- Checkout Darrin Zeer's book, *Office Spa: Stress Relief for the Working Week*, 2002, for good relaxation techniques.

MISTAKE 55 – *HAVE AN OUTDATED RESUME*

Tom C., an insurance underwriter, learned the hard way about not keeping his resume updated. As he puts it:

"I'm great with numbers and landed my dream job about a year after graduating college. The job let me use my analytical skills and I was part of an accounting department that enjoyed working together. Over the years, I was able to take additional classes that helped me gain Project Management knowledge and experience.

Then, this newly created position opened up and I was a perfect candidate for it. The problem was that I saw the internal posting on the due date because I had just returned from vacation. Human Resources required a current resume in order to be considered for the position. I had not updated my resume in at least five years. So, I lost out on a wonderful opportunity to use my project management skills."

If you have just started with a company, the idea of updating your resume may be the furthest thing from your mind. But, you are the only one truly vested in your own career. You cannot expect your employer to remember every training class you took or if you completed a degree.

Keep in mind the following when outlining your job duties and accomplishments under the Work Experience section of your resume:
- Highlight your most important job responsibilities first.
- Use action phrases and keep grammatical tenses appropriate.
- Incorporate tangible results.
- Use bullets to draw attention to your achievements.

TIPS:
- Update your resume annually with significant contributions you achieved during the past 12-months; especially certifications relevant to your current position or one you want to attain.
- Keep track of the quantifiable results you have achieved. How much cost savings? Increased efficiency? Vendor negotiations?
- Get a professional resume review every 4-5 years to keep current on trends.

MISTAKE 56 – *DON'T LEAD THROUGH A CRISIS*

In the normal course of meeting with managers, there is more and more talk of failure – from the global economic situation to what is directly going on in their company. It feels like there is an energy shift from hopelessness to downright panic.

These corporate leaders are smart, talented, and highly capable in their positions. Yet, some are terrified about making it through the current market uncertainties. You do need to create a personal environment which nurtures your mind so you have the capacity to lead from the heart.

HOW TO LEAD THROUGH A CRISIS

1. **Communicate** – During stressful situations, your team needs to know what is going on. Stop the gossip and rumor mill from starting by giving truthful information regularly.
2. **Be Visible** – Get out of your office and be available for questions as they come up. Your employees will crave answers even if you don't have them. This is a good opportunity to address their concerns and calm any fears.
3. **Use Self-Control** – Your own behavior is magnified during a crisis. People are watching your reactions to the situation and deciphering fact from fiction. Watch out for high-emotion words you speak and your body language.

Ultimately, you need to create a sense of order even if you do not have all the answers. Leadership isn't easy and leadership is very public. You need courage, faith, and vision to make it through the difficult periods so your team is stronger for the experience.

TIPS:
- Stop ingesting daily negativity. Give yourself a break by turning off the TV and radio for a week.
- Get your message out using different media (voicemail, email, employee newsletter, staff meetings, roundtable discussions, Intranet).

MISTAKE 57 – *BAD HABITS*

I have a sign on my desk that reads, "Let go of those things that no longer serve you." Think about that statement long enough and you will come up with dozens of interpretations. Today, contemplate all the bad habits that don't work for you.

Do any of these sound familiar? You:
- Have trouble returning phone calls on time.
- Are late for meetings and appointments.
- Lack clarity about expected outcomes, monthly targets, goals, etc.
- Avoid paperwork.
- Take work home with you.

The good news is that each of these habits can be broken. The more difficult news is that it will require you to change. Your work life right this minute did not just happen to you. It is all about the choices you made and how you responded to each situation.

A habit is something you do so often it becomes easy; a behavior you keep repeating. Up to 90% of our normal behavior is based on habits. We have a tendency to call this our "routine" and there are some folks who enjoy the ritual of their routines. However, if that routine – that habit – no longer serves you then it is time to exchange it for one that will.

3 STEPS TO CHANGE BAD HABITS INTO GOOD HABITS:

Step 1: Be Conscious of the Habits Not Working For You.
Step 2: Identify the New Habit You Want in Your Life.
Step 3: Create and Implement an Action Plan for the New Habit.

TIPS:
- When identifying the new habit in your life, make the benefits so compelling that they spur you into action.
- Change is not always easy. Do not give up! Give yourself some grace as you develop into the manager you want to be.

MISTAKE 58 – *DON'T BUILD A TEAM IDENTITY*

There is a wide interpretation in what managers call a "team." It could mean anything from a bunch of people sitting in the same vicinity to a highly functioning group working toward common goals.

Some managers mistakenly think that creating their teams' identity extends to selecting a team name and roster. However, to be taken seriously by your organization you need to cultivate these seven leadership qualities to fully integrate a strong identity. (Adapted from 'The Emotionally Intelligent Team,' (Marcia Hughes and James Bradford Terrell, 2007)

1. **Sense of purpose** – Teams need to know what they are supposed to do, how success will be measured, clear staff agendas, and how their work impacts the bottom-line. You need agreement on why the team exists.
2. **Acceptance of one another** – It is unrealistic to expect everyone on the team to like each other. However, it is essential that all team members show mutual respect and support in spite of any differences.
3. **Perception that the team is a distinct entity** – Watch out for language such as "sort of a team" or "kind of a team" or "like a team." If you start hearing this, then you have not clearly defined the purpose of the team.
4. **Commitment** – How do you know that each team member is committed to your team? Managers need to help the team identify how they know that each member is committed through the successes and setbacks.
5. **Pride** – Pay attention to how you speak about being part of the team. Are you embarrassed and want to hide? Or, pleased to be associated with the other team members and the work you are doing?
6. **Clarity about roles and responsibilities** – Each team member needs to know their role or function and what they are responsible for producing. Knowing your job description is merely a starting point.
7. **Resilience** – Buoyancy, the ability to flex, to bounce, to shift is paramount with the rapid pace of change. Teams who can quickly "read" their business and customers and adapt are profoundly inspiring.

TIPS:
- Solicit suggestions from team members on what they believe is their team identity.
- Keep in mind the degree to which individuals identify with the team shapes its strength and productivity.

MISTAKE 59 – *NEED TO BE RIGHT*

On three separate occasions this past week, I noticed the disregard people have for someone else's feelings without understanding the context of the situation. Each interaction had in common:

- One person getting admonished.
- Little, if any, two-way dialogue.
- The instigator becoming more aggressive in their need to have the last word.

How Can You Be Kind Instead of Being Right?

What does being a servant-leader mean to you in today's business climate? Working in an environment where your own needs are ranked first. Needs to meet goals, quotas, targets, and budgets (being right) may have you blinded to the needs of others on your team (being kind).

Are you rewarding a team through incentives, bonuses, raises, additional benefits, or promotion possibility? While these approaches can be effective they are also limiting over the long-term. Simply, they fail to inspire. You may be following company policy and seeing results using these methods, but what is being said about your leadership ability?

Your choice: To be a respected manager achieving organizational goals or to be a treasured servant-leader focused on genuine connection to each individual at a heart level.

Being Kind: Nice, thoughtful, compassionate, humane, considerate, understanding.
Being Right: Correct, accurate, exact, precise, absolute, total.

TIPS:
- To create a genuine connection (being kind), ask yourself, "Who am I serving right now? My ego or the soul of another?"
- Create an intentional team sanctuary. Sanctuary means being loyal to each other behind your backs.

MISTAKE 60 – *ETHICAL DILEMMAS*

You have probably heard the statement, "Just do the right thing." It sounds simple yet many times figuring out what the "right thing" to do is very difficult. The business world is far from black and white, and managers are asked to make decisions concerning the "gray" areas.

Navigating your way through what is right versus wrong is not something to be taken lightly. It requires you to be grounded in a set of values and ideals which you can confidently voice.

WHAT DO YOU BELIEVE?

Honest answers to the following questions will help you define your moral compass. Consider:
- How clear am I of my own vision and values?
- How do my values align with organizational values?
- How will I handle discontentment, mistakes, and setbacks?
- How solid is my relationship with my team?
- How can I keep myself motivated and encouraged?
- Am I the right person to be leading at this very moment? Why?
- How prepared am I to handle the problems that face my team?
- What are my beliefs about how the team ought to conduct business?

Once you have answered these questions – and those that arise from your initial answers – you have the foundation from which to make decisions in the gray areas of your work.

3 KEYS TO ETHICAL LEADERSHIP

1. **Know yourself** – You have already answered the previous questions. Go further by evaluating to what degree you are open to compromising certain beliefs.
2. **Know your team** – Not everyone on your team will think or believe exactly like you. Provide them with enough information about who you are as a person. Let them know your hot buttons - those unshakeable beliefs on which you do not compromise.
3. **Know your organization** – Determine how closely your personal values align with your company. A rule of thumb: The more closely aligned you are, the greater your job satisfaction. Why? You won't need to put up a façade if you agree with the belief. You will, however, need to decide how to support those areas around which you do disagree. A good place to

start is to have a conversation with your manager. Sometimes, there is leeway between the "letter of the law" and the "spirit of the law."

TIPS:
- Remember, ethics requires you to hold a conviction that what you are doing enhances the team by balancing your needs with that of the entire group.
- Visit www.78ManagerMistakes.com to receive a complimentary Values Checklist. Click on the FREE RESOURCES tab and download the *Values Checklist*.

MISTAKE 61 – *ALWAYS BE SERIOUS*

Are you regularly allowing your team time to re-energize during the day? Employees cannot always be working if you want them to be creative and productive.

The idea of **corporate play** has been around for a few years. Research indicates the following benefits of adding "play" into corporate life:
1. It breaks down barriers between individuals.
2. It highlights the multiplicity of skills within the set team.
3. It furthers interpersonal relationships and creates an ambience that welcomes different working styles.
4. It identifies the self-motivation and behavioral characteristics of the teams that perform well.
5. It develops strong team spirit.

INCORPORATING PLAY INTO YOUR TEAM

Do involve everyone. Ask yourself:
1. Are there play opportunities geared toward all team members?
2. Does every play activity keep team members safe mentally, emotionally, and physically?
3. Are all members participating when our team is playing?

Do keep it FUN. Ask:
1. Does this play activity reflect well on our team and the company?
2. What no-cost, simple, and creative play can we do in under 5 minutes?
3. Will this activity reduce team stress through laughter?

Do actively participate. Ask yourself:
1. Am I joining team play for all activities or only the ones I enjoy?
2. Am I interacting with the same team members during the activity or connecting with everyone?
3. Am I enjoying the company of team members and not judging their performance?

TIPS:
- Building genuine relationship with your team includes regular time-outs for play.
- Do a quick team member survey to get their suggestions for incorporating play into the team, best day/time, how regularly, and what activities they would be willing to participate in.

MISTAKE 62 – *BE A ROGUE LEADER*

Sarah Palin's book, *Going Rogue*, got me thinking about rogue leaders within organizations. You know the person – it's the employee who went "off the deep end" because none of his decisions and actions were consistent with the organizations goals.

The rogue leader is a person of influence who begins to deviate from agreed upon objectives, departs from company endorsed ideals, and defies established ethical standards. It's easier to identify the blatant behavior, but sometimes "going rogue" takes on a subtle form and is easily missed.

You could argue that the rogue leader is to blame for intentionally sabotaging the organization. But, is that the truth? Perhaps he simply misunderstood the objectives and is acting without harmful intent.

Are we talking about someone else or perhaps **you** are the rogue leader? Let's check. It could be **you** if:

- Senior management is treating you differently.
- Your team is off track on reaching goals.
- Human Resources is receiving more complaints about you.
- Work is being redirected away from you.
- No one solicits your advice.
- Resources are becoming even more scarce.

Rogue leadership is destructive and undermines the mission of the entire organization. You simply cannot have one person running off in one direction while the rest of your team is pulling in another. Decide if you care enough about the organization, and your team, to align with their vision, mission, and values.

TIPS:
- Ask yourself: Is my behavior helping or hurting the team? Decide by measuring it against your business goals and objectives.
- Verify what expectations you are operating under. If everyone else is working toward the same goal except you, you cannot use "I didn't know" as an excuse.

MISTAKE 63 – *POMPOSITY*

It's been said that the only thing you really have in today's workplace is your reputation. Some managers take great pride in the good reputation they have built. Others revel in showing off extremely bad behavior.

Some time back I read an article by David Ellis, CEO of Tenneco, where he described executive pomposity and the affect it had in his organization. The term "pomposity" has stuck with me because of the visual images it brings to mind. It is, simply, letting authority go to your head. Left unchecked it can breed a sense of entitlement which will alienate you from both clients and your team. While pomposity may inflate your ego, it deflates others around you.

Whether you like it or not, organizations have a hierarchy to which you need to pay attention. The corporate values and culture will dictate how you handle the privileges in your position.

It is rare to always work for an employer whose values mimic yours. As a manager, however, you are asked to uphold those values for your team regardless of your personal views. You may not be able to voice dissatisfaction with your organization, but you can make little changes that have a great impact on moving the culture from hierarchal to one of collaboration and inclusion.

3 KEYS TO OVERCOMING LEADERSHIP POMPOSITY

1. Keep yourself accessible.
2. Don't think more of yourself than you do of those around you.
3. Always share the credit and take full responsibility for all outcomes.

In the words of Mwai Kibaki, "Leadership is a privilege to better the lives of others. It is not an opportunity to satisfy personal greed."

TIPS:
- To avoid pomposity, be available to others to see more perspectives than your own. Try in-person conversations, monthly Town Hall meetings, Brown Bag lunches, or a quarterly department social event.
- Reflect on how you can better the lives of those around you. Then do one of those things.

MISTAKE 64 – *LACK OF SELF MANAGEMENT*

Believe me when I say, there will come a time when you totally lose your cool at work. Perhaps a team member just cursed out your best customer. Or, your company restructured and you've been demoted.

How you react in the moment of receiving horrific news determines the willingness of your team to acknowledge you as their manager. Are they embarrassed by your behavior or proud of how you handled the situation?

Here's the story of "Jane" who immediately elected to stay with her company after being reassigned to her old job. In a few days, Jane became so furious she started looking dumber with each passing day. She elected to stay mad and started making more and more irrational decisions as time passed. She admitted:

1. the job had become too much to handle.
2. the overtime was causing stress at home.
3. she hates employee excuses ("Why am I their babysitter?").
4. not keeping her boss informed or updated on projects or issues.

Simply, Jane was not given an explanation of **why** this change was necessary, and her imagination spun stories and tall tales to counter the blow to her ego. She reacted badly and was not in control of her emotions. Her outbursts were seen by upper management as confirmation that their demotion of Jane was appropriate.

IF THIS HAPPENS TO YOU

1. Manage your bruised ego.
- Don't talk to anyone until you have given yourself time to reflect.
- Don't burn any bridges by getting angry.
- Don't make any rash decisions. Sort through your options.
- Deal with negative feelings sooner rather than later.

2. Find out the real reason the decision was made.
- Confront any weaknesses or challenges and work to build skills in those areas.
- Is it a company restructuring or is it your personal performance? This answer will tell you if you still have a career with the company.
- Honestly assess how you enjoy your job. Does it seem overwhelming? Empty? Get to your truth so you can make the necessary changes.

- Stay composed through whatever you hear. Do not try to defend your actions at this point. Listen and ask open-ended questions for full understanding by getting all the details.

3. Decide if you want the scaled-back job.
- Are you better suited to this job?
- Are you close to being vested with the company?
- Do you enjoy your co-workers?
- Do you still believe in the company vision, mission, and values?

TIPS:
- Remember, perks come and go but only you are responsible for your career. Take control and create your own job security.
- Seek outside counseling if you need more help in working through your feelings over emotional ties. Check with Human Resources to see if you are eligible to participate in the Employee Assistance Program.

MISTAKE 65 – *PERFECTIONISM*

Repeat after me: "Good is good enough." Striving for excellence is a good thing. Striving to be perfect is not. It borders on obsession. Unless your job requires being 100% perfect, give yourself a break. Yes, have high standards but be realistic and flexible.

Good managers have sabotaged their performance because they fixated on doing such a quality job they over-produced the end product. Too much time was wasted on re-working insignificant details. Case in point: One manager rewrote her own meeting notes twice because "they didn't look neat enough."

Time management guru, David Allen, in his book *Getting Things Done* promotes a 5-Step Process for increasing your productivity: (1) Collect, (2) Process, (3) Organize, (4) Review, (5) Do

I have taught employees office organization and time management principles for years. How is it that the task from today's To Do List keeps popping up weeks from now? Practice using these tips:
1. Start with a pile and deal with only one item at a time.
2. Only touch a piece of paper once.
3. If something requires action – do it, delegate it, or defer it.
4. If it does not require action – file it, toss it, or hold it for later.
5. Give everything a "place" in your office.
6. Create a tickler file.
7. Track projects with chronological files, waiting for action items, etc.
8. Keep a calendar and record everything.

KEYS TO GETTING THINGS DONE

1. Take personal responsibility for everything.
2. Make a decision to "Just Do It."

TIPS:
- Face all your objections head on. Ask yourself, "Honestly, what is the worst that could happen?" Look at the realities of the situation not what is in your imagination.
- You can get more done in a 15-minute highly concentrated block of time being completely focused on a small task of a bigger project. The trick is to break down the project into manageable chunks.

MISTAKE 66 – *DON'T INVOLVE STAFF REGULARLY*

An easy way to get everyone involved is to have a brainstorming session. Have you been doing them correctly? Let's find out…

Brainstorming Ground Rules:
- Record every idea exactly as it was stated. Don't evaluate ideas.
- Don't discuss ideas until the clarifying step (See Step 5 below).
- Wild ideas are encouraged. Use your imagination.
- Build on other's ideas (combine, expand, piggyback).
- Go for quantity – more is better. Repetition is okay here.
- Don't quit too soon. When ideas start to slow down, ask, "What else?"

Purpose: To generate lots of ideas in a short period of time; encourage creativity.

Time Needed: 10 - 30 minutes (depending on group size; number of ideas)

Brainstorming Steps:
STEP 1 Clarify the challenge OR ask a key question. Write it on a flipchart or whiteboard.
STEP 2 Review / establish ground rules – see above.
STEP 3 Have participants shout out ideas and capture them on a flipchart. Accept all ideas. Write the idea exactly the way it was spoken. (It may be helpful to have two flipcharts and two scribes to capture all the ideas.)
STEP 4 Build on ideas. Keep the creative process going.

AFTER THE LIST HAS BEEN GENERATED:

STEP 5 Clarify each idea – seek more information. Now is the time for discussion!
STEP 6 Eliminate duplicate ideas – do not combine at this point.
STEP 7 Now start making some decisions around the remaining ideas:
- Eliminate any unrealistic ideas (cannot be achieved due to lack of time, funding, or management buy-in)
- Prioritize remaining ideas (team decides on priority criteria – for example, easiest to complete in next 30 days)

TIPS:
- Set a goal such as 75 ideas. Often the best ideas are the last ones.
- Rotate the role of scribe so everyone is involved in the process.

MISTAKE 67 – *MANIPULATE*

The Merriam-Webster dictionary defines the word manipulate as:
"…to control or play upon by artful, unfair, or insidious means especially to one's own advantage."

Many workplaces have at least one person who is aggressive, selfish, pushy, and only concerned with getting his or her own way rather than doing their job. In any organization, you do not want to be that manipulative manager. Being manipulative, a bully, is self-centered behavior that can be stressful, reduce productivity and create management problems.

Manipulative behavior can take the following forms:
- Whining
- Making others feel guilty
- Using passive-aggressive tactics
- Demeaning others by making fun of them
- Using inappropriate humor
- Taking a martyr approach
- Speaking malicious gossip
- Taking control of conversations
- Becoming the center of attention

Manipulation is about two things: (1) getting your own way and (2) getting control and power.

TIPS:
- Never threaten, yell at, or use physical intimidation toward another employee.
- Understand and abide by workplace policies. They are there for the protection of all.
- During meetings, use proper meeting management techniques to avoid blaming others, aggressive behavior, and monopolizing the floor.
- When handling disputes, focus on solving the problem or addressing the issue, not figuring out who is at fault.
- Attend communication training with emphasis on appropriate workplace assertive behavior.

MISTAKE 68 – *DON'T CREATE A LIFE PLAN*

I coach many managers who have intricate goals and plans for their team. Some plans are complicated; some even works of art. These managers do it right. They share their vision, collaborate with their team on tactical goals, and give daily encouragement so team members always perform at their best.

Few of these brilliant managers are truly living their dream life. They have put so much energy into their career, a new home, or even a vacation that many end up discouraged and disillusioned because they failed to plan for something more important – their life.

You can live your life **on purpose**. How? Begin by creating your Life Plan. This will help you become an active participant in your life instead of wondering how life passed you by. Your Life Plan will:
- Keep you on track with family, friends, and career.
- Serve as a map to get back on the path when you deviate.
- Allow for intentional accountability when shared with a mentor or coach.

3 STEPS TO CREATING YOUR LIFE PLAN

STEP 1 – *Outcomes*
STEP 2 – *Priorities*
STEP 3 – *Action Plans*

STEP 1 – Outcomes. How do you want to be remembered? Fast forward to the end of your life and look back in order to answer the question. Suggestions on areas of focus include family, friends, colleagues, work, community, God, and health to name a few.

STEP 2 – Priorities. Answer the question, "What is important to me?" Identify and prioritize all the areas in your life you feel are important to you. For example, career, immediate family, finances, personal development, health, and volunteering. Prioritizing these areas will highlight where you are currently out of balance. For example, is your career going great but you never see your kids?

STEP 3 – Action Plans. Plans are great but will never get you where you want to be unless you take action. In this step, you reflect on each area and think through where you are and where you want to be.

For each of your priority areas from Step 2, break down each one into four parts:

1. **Purpose Statement** – State what your purpose is within this area.
2. **Future Vision** – Describe exactly how you envision yourself in each of these areas in the future. I recommend projecting out 1-year, 3-years, 5-years. This will take a bit more work, but it's worth taking the time to state where you see yourself. Write out your Future Vision in the present tense, like it is already a reality.
3. **Current Reality** – State exactly where you are today in relationship to your Future Vision. Be brutally honest with yourself. Helpful hints:
   - The more honest you are, the more progress you will see.
   - List things as they first come to mind; don't over-analyze.
   - Use bullet points as you do this "brain dump."
   - Be so personal and honest with yourself that you would be embarrassed if anyone else read it. (Remember, no one sees this unless you ask to be held accountable by someone you trust.)
4. **Commitments** – List specific actions you will take in order to move from your Current Reality to your Future Vision. In other words, what will you do on a daily basis to get you closer to your goal?

You will need to dig deep, and it will take some time when you first begin. This activity is not for the faint-hearted manager.

What does creating your Life Plan have to do with managing a team? It is when you think long and hard about your life and where it is going that you become more satisfied in general. And, when you are satisfied with the direction it affects your management style and impacts those you lead.

TIPS:
- Set aside time to systematically design the outcomes you want to see in the major areas of your life. **You** decide what major areas to include.
- There is not a rule that says you cannot keep modifying your Life Plan through the years as circumstances change.
- Complimentary download of *My Life Plan* at www.78ManagerMistakes.com, click on FREE RESOURCES tab.

MISTAKE 69 – *OVER-RELIANCE ON TECHNOLOGY*

The speed of technology is rapidly increasing. Just a couple years ago the iPhone was the latest-and-greatest improvement. The 2010 introduction of Apple's iPad will be obsolete soon enough.

Technology is good. It allows us to communicate faster, solve problems quicker, immediately relay data to customers, and virtually connect across the globe.

Technology is bad, however, when you have an over-reliance on it and ignore face-to-face interpersonal work relationships.

The Millenial Generation (born from 1977-1997) thrives on technology and the vast majority are experts at integrating multiple forms into the workplace. They can create highly collaborative and self-directed communities through the use of social media, crowd sourcing, instant messaging, podcasts, and videos to name a few modalities.

Yet, they may not be as adept at holding a conversation with the person sitting next to them or giving a client presentation.

TIPS:
- If you are technically savvy, trade your technical knowledge with a colleague to learn more verbal communication skills you may lack.
- The high-performance and speak-your-mind philosophy are two characteristics of the Millenial Generation. If you are in this generation, give team members some grace as they begin to embrace emerging workplace technology. It will take some time for them to change.

MISTAKE 70 – *UNTIMELY PERFORMANCE REVIEWS*

"About once a week, I get out of my office and spend some time walking around different departments so employees don't always see Human Resources as the "police." I take a notebook with me to jot down notes in case I'm unable to answer their question immediately.

One of our accounting clerks was celebrating her one year anniversary with us, and I happened to wander through her area on the anniversary date. She stopped to ask when she would be receiving a review. She went on to say that her manager had never talked to her about how she was doing since the day she was hired. The manager had not completed the employee's 90-day, 6-month, or annual review.

The best way to lose a good employee is to show your lack of care by ignoring their work. When I questioned the manager, he said getting a review done on time did not matter because retroactive pay had always been approved in the past."

- Anonymous, Banking, Brookfield, WI

If you want to truly create a positive environment, then you need to:
- involve employees in setting clear goals and objectives.
- coach employees when they request help.
- monitor employee progress towards goals and give feedback.
- provide adequate training and resources.
- recognize employees for good performance.
- tell everyone on your team how you will evaluate performance.
- tackle poor performance head-on.

TIPS:
- Schedule in your planner when you will have formal performance discussions with each employee. A minimum of two, near their anniversary and 6-months after, is a general recommendation.
- Supplement formal discussion with daily feedback and coaching.

MISTAKE 71 – *DON'T DEAL WITH DIFFICULT PEOPLE*

You will work with all kinds of personalities during your career. The more adept you become at handling different types of people; the more skilled you are at communication and getting your message across. One of your responsibilities is paying attention to individual behaviors, and identifying them for documentation purposes. Let's look at five common difficult behavior types:

TYPE	TACTIC THEY USE
Constant Critic	Extremely negative; a nitpicker and complainer who commonly uses put-downs and insults with team members about their "incompetence".
Two-headed Snake	A dishonest style; pretending to be nice, while sabotaging the targeted team member.
Gatekeeper	Likes to be in control at all times; commonly making up new rules on a whim, deliberately cutting team members out of the communication loop and then giving them the silent treatment.
Screaming Mimi	Controls through fear and intimidation; impulsive, explosive, and overbearing.
Constant Complainer	Nothing is ever right, good enough, or going their way.

When faced with these personalities here is what to do to minimize tension:
- Be more tolerant and accepting of others and differing viewpoints.
- Ask the other person to talk about their point-of-view and their wants and needs.
- Show support by using active listening skills (paraphrasing; empathy).

TIPS:
- Use assertive skills to communicate your viewpoint.
- Don't take out your own emotions on others; find appropriate ways to vent.

MISTAKE 72 – *TELL EVERYONE YOU'RE IN CHARGE*

Trust me, on your first day at work everyone on your new team will know who the new manager is. News travels fast when the position is filled, and do not be surprised if they started doing reconnaissance before you even stepped foot through the door.

It is easier these days to gather information from a variety of sources using the Internet. If you have posted a recent picture in your profile, your new team will recognize you. You do not have to make a big show about being The Boss. Simply show them how you will make a positive difference. Your actions will speak louder than any words.

TIPS:
- Monitor both your personal and professional information on social websites. Only post content you would not mind the new staff knowing.
- Prepare several great questions to ask your new team members about themselves.
- Remember to focus on them; not your greatness.

MISTAKE 73 – *THINK YOU CAN MANAGE YOUR FRIENDS*

Marge Foster, Store Manager, Clothestime, Atlanta, GA, relates her experience:

"After six months as a sales clerk in a retail clothing store, I was promoted to a manager position. I now was in a position of managing the staff that had become my friends. My mistake was letting things slide when my friends asked for a favor.

It started out innocently enough with the occasional "coming in late." I asked them not to do it often, and they always promised it wouldn't happen again.

It did.

It was very difficult to separate personal friendship from business. I still had goals to meet, and felt they were taking advantage of our relationship. There is a fine line between how to keep your distance but still be friendly. I learned to be cordial but not too familiar.

I must have found the right balance. Several years later at a different clothing company, I was asked to help open new stores in the southeast US based on the performance of managing my own store location."

TIPS:
- Create Guiding Principles for your department within the first few weeks of your new position. These will be the operating rules of how the team interacts and treats each other on a daily basis.
- Do not get offended if you are no longer included in water-cooler discussions. It does not mean the staff doesn't like you. It means they recognize you as their manager.

MISTAKE 74 – *BE EFFICIENT VS. EFFECTIVE*

A big factor in your promotion was, most likely, your excellent technical ability to do the job. Somewhere along the way you demonstrated your skills and abilities.

"Technical" job duties vary depending on the industry. The duties may have involved running equipment, creating reports and spreadsheets, or quality control. These kinds of tasks can be redesigned to be completed faster, cheaper, or more streamlined. That is efficiency.

In your manager role, you have a new set of "technical" duties. These can include creating the staffing calendar, writing an annual review, or facilitating staff meetings. Learning these duties are important.

There are also "interpersonal" duties you need to master. These align to the people-side of your job. It's the other half of your overall responsibilities. Interpersonal activities are things like giving feedback, coaching, and helping staff members resolve conflict, to name a few.

Whenever you need to handle the human-side of your job, how effective you are becomes important. Effectiveness has to do with doing the right thing; efficiency has to do with getting things done fast. When working with people, effectiveness is rarely efficient.

TIPS:
- The best "people" results come when you take the necessary time in the relationship to do things right.
- Bring the whole team together when working on making processes and procedures efficient.

MISTAKE 75 – *INABILITY TO REFUSE EMPLOYEE REQUESTS*

Let's face it – you want to be the "good guy" with your employees, right? There is satisfaction in being able to say "Yes" to a request; to be a valuable resource. But, what happens when you need to decline a heart-felt appeal? How do you refuse an employee request without creating resentment?

Resentment is not good because it destroys relationships. It builds a wall and does not allow for open communication. Obviously, a resentful atmosphere is not conducive to building collaborative, successful teams.

There are methods you can use when you simply must reject a request. My assumption is you have a valid reason for not allowing the request based on business needs.

THREE TECHNIQUES TO REFUSE A REQUEST

1. **Use Tact** – Being tactful may be difficult to learn, but it allows you to avoid unnecessary conflict.
2. **Say "NO"** – Understand exactly what is being requested before you respond; explain in detail why the request cannot be granted; be firm when saying "No." Eliminate the word try.
3. **Be Sincere** – Demonstrate your concern and make your personal regret believable. Sincerity takes time to nurture so don't worry if you've been inconsistent.

TIPS:
- Act the same way alone as you do in the presence of others. This is the real you; the person that people will trust.
- Sincerity exposes you. Remain calm and non-confrontational when faced with employee reactions.

MISTAKE 76 – *DON'T EXPECT THE DARK SIDE OF MANAGEMENT*

The idea of a "dark side" of management may seem foreign to you because it is rarely a topic of conversation. Why? Inside each of us is a "dark side" – those parts we usually keep hidden from others. It is the ugliness of a personality trait that we do not want uncovered. But, let's talk about it.

A dark side usually comes on when you are under stress and your guard is down. During this time, you exhibit self-defeating behaviors which interfere with working relationships, team effectiveness, and organizational goals. Left unchecked, your dark side can alienate colleagues and undermine trust and commitment.

Your dark side may reveal itself through:
- Allowing conflicts of interest.
- Unethical practices becoming the norm.
- Sloppy decision-making.
- Avoidance of co-workers.
- Colluding with clients.

TIPS:
- Evaluate all your emotional responses, especially when under pressure. (See Mistake #38 for more information on Emotional Intelligence.)
- Be aware of your own perception of your behavior versus others' perception of your behavior. For example, you may see yourself as enthusiastic and confident yet others may see you as volatile and arrogant.
- Always have a coach. Receiving honest and confidential feedback regularly from an outside source will help you understand yourself better over time.
- Have at least one personal development goal in your annual performance plan.

MISTAKE 77 – *RESIST CHANGE*

Taking a risk means you change something from the status quo. You are doing something different than what is expected – expectations from yourself and the team.
If whatever you do is not working, you need to be flexible. You must change your action plan if the current one does not produce the required results. If you want your team to change, support the risk you are about to take, you must be prepared to make the first step yourself.

REASONS FOR WORKPLACE RESISTANCE TO CHANGE

- **Fear of the unknown.** Change implies uncertainty, and uncertainty is uncomfortable.
- **Fear of failure.** Doing something new or different may require skill and abilities that are beyond current employee capabilities.
- **Disagreement with the need for change.** Employees may feel you are going in the wrong direction.
- **Losing something of value.** Employees want to know how making the change will affect them personally. If they believe they will lose something, expect them to resist your plan.
- **Leaving a comfort zone.** Employees may be afraid to follow a leaders' new project/suggestion because it would force them to stretch their comfort zones.
- **Misunderstanding and lack of trust.** Employees resist change when they don't understand the implications of not taking the risk, and perceive that it might cost them more than they would gain.
- **Inertia.** All organizations suffer various degrees of inertia and try to maintain the status quo. Much effort is required to make changes which can lead to employee burnout.

TIPS:
- If the majority of the team is resisting changes you suggest, this is typically the case when there is a lack of trust between you and the team members.
- Most people don't like change because they don't like being changed. Educate them with information on the reason the change is needed.

MISTAKE 78 – STAY TOO LONG AT THE "PARTY"

I realize you are new to management. However, there will come a day when you decide to leave your organization. Will you know how to handle it? Have you experienced any of these?

- You dread Sunday night because you are facing another long week at work.
- You have an increase in illnesses the past 6 months.
- You cry in the shower getting ready for work.

What was once a promising job in a great company has changed, and you no longer enjoy the work. It may have happened quickly or circumstances accumulated over years. This change affects employees at all levels in the organization, and is more noticeable when you are in a leadership position.

You know it is time to move on when your boss no longer supports you and you cannot back the organization whole-heartedly. If your boss no longer "loves" you, then be proactive in assessing where you went wrong and decide if it can be fixed.

Managers often find it especially hard to leave when they have poured their soul into creating a team. If you find yourself in this situation, remember these Do's and Don'ts to keep the connection with your own team during your transition.

WHAT TO DO

1. **Create an interim plan.** Update the documentation you are passing along to your replacement.
2. **Ask the team to support the transition.** Advise your group early of your departure and work through their various emotions.
3. **Show your kindness and gratitude.** Take the higher road by showing empathy toward team members, your boss, and the organization.
4. **Maintain your confidence and energy.** Remain actively engaged in how the team is meeting goals through your last day.
5. **Celebrate with the team.** Folks will want to acknowledge your impact on the team.

WHAT NOT TO DO

1. **Forget your customers.** Customers are the life-blood of your organization. Reassure them the company is prepared to handle any minor disruption your departure may create. Introduce them to your replacement, if possible.
2. **Vent.** Do not speak badly about your boss or the organization.
3. **Cut and run.** Do not take confidential or competitive information from the organization as you are walking out the door.
4. **Steal the best.** Do not approach the "best" team members and offer to take them with you to the next company. If you had the skill to create one successful team, you can do it again elsewhere.

TIPS:
- Your character is what will be remembered. Your last impression is just as significant as the initial impression that got you hired.
- Make sure all your work is up-to-date and current so the incoming manager can pick up where you left off.

AFTERWORD

Each of the mistakes presented are filled with truth. I have seen dozens of well-meaning managers get unnecessarily sidetracked because they were not coached early in their career. They began their management responsibilities with fervor and excitement only to be blind-sided by a corporate decision to reassign or terminate them. I, too, have been that manager.

It is from experience and courageously asking a trusted colleague for mentoring that I regained confidence in my abilities to manage people. It was a heart-wrenching process and, oh so, needed. If my decision to drop the ego, ask for specific training, get coaching, and implement recommendations had not been made, I would not have been able to authentically teach these principles, through individual coaching, seminars, and in the organizations where I consult.

I know that without practicing these techniques and strategies I could never have written this book. If I didn't practice daily what I preach, I wouldn't have a successful business or the privilege of serving the clients I do.

This isn't the end. Missing is the detailed nitty-gritty HOW-TO for each of the mistakes made by other managers. Team Fusion stands in service to help you overcome any skill gaps through coaching and training.

The more you bring good management principles into your work relationships, the more positively you affect the people and organizations you work for. Imagine what your legacy would be like if you incorporated a holistic approach into your management style and philosophy today.

Jack Welch said, "Before you are a leader, success is all about growing yourself. When you become a leader, success is all about growing others."

My hope for you is that you grow into a leader who influences the people you care about most to make this a richer life.

WORKSHOPS AND TEAMBUILDING EVENTS

Create a High Performing Workplace by bringing Marjorie to Your Organization!

CUSTOMIZED LEARNING AT YOUR SITE:

Programs range from 2 hours to a full day depending on your objectives. Clients use our physical adventures for:

- Leader development
- Encouraging team communication
- Creative problem-solving
- Fostering teamwork and collaboration
- Improving planning and execution skills
- Sales meetings
- Client networking events
- Employee summer outings

We offer over 70 different team-building events to energize and reward your team. Here is a small sampling of what we can deliver: Outdoor or Indoor Events, Team Trainings, Scavenger and Treasure Hunts, Philanthropic Events, and Culinary Events.

SAMPLE TEAM TRAININGS:

- Communicating Across the Generations
- Developing and Leading a Team
- Creative Thinking & Problem Solving
- Conflict Resolution Made Practical
- Delivering an Effective Presentation

Call or go online for details!

www.TeamFusion.net

marjorie@teamfusion.net | 414-477-6655 phone | 414-386-1717 fax

COACHING/MENTORING

Continuing Education Enrollment Form

"Okay Marjorie, I'm tired of wasting time and I'm Ready to Have You Right There to Help ME Avoid the Mistakes That Can Stall My Career. I'm tired of watching less qualified people get promoted before me, and know there's got to be an easier way. I'm ready and committed to TAKE ACTION!"

Name:_____
Tel #:_____ Email:_____ Fax:_____
Address:_____
City:_____ State:_____ Zip:_____
Print name as it appears on card:_____
Credit card number:_____
Card (circle): Visa   M/C   Expiration Date:_____
I authorize the amount below to be charged to the above credit card:

Signature:_____ Date:_____
(Required for credit card authorizations)

Mark Your Option: (These are 2010 rates. Call for current investment options.)

☐ *Option 1* ($1,497) *:* 3-Month Coaching/Mentoring Program with Marjorie
(Easy Payment Plan of $499 Per Month)

☐ *Option 2* ($2,496) *:* 6-Month Coaching/Mentoring Program with Marjorie
(Easy Payment Plan of $416 Per Month)

☐ *Option 3* ($3,996) *:* 12-Month Coaching/Mentoring Program with Marjorie
(Easy Payment Plan of $333 Per Month)

You Receive:
- Four (4) 30-minute coaching calls per month
- One (1) 30-minute Strategic Career Planning call
- One (1) 30-minute Leadership Launch call with the 12-month Program
- Weekly e-newsletter, Team Talk Today
- COMPLEMENTARY 30-minute 'Get Acquainted' Coaching Session

---

www.TeamFusion.net
marjorie@teamfusion.net | 414-477-6655 phone | 414-386-1717 fax

Please **EMAIL** to:
marjorie@TeamFusion.net

or **FAX** to:
414-386-1717

KEYNOTE SPEECHES

Inspire Your Managers!

Marjorie Treu is CEO of Marjorie Speaks, a company dedicated to empowering managers with the tools to create and live their leadership legacy. Her career has led Marjorie into the worlds of travel, banking, retail, healthcare, non-profits, and manufacturing. The challenges facing today's executives are similar regardless of industry:

- Lack of visionary leadership in succession planning.
- Low employee morale during uncertain economic times.
- Limited understanding of generational differences in the workplace.

MOST REQUESTED KEYNOTE TOPICS:

1. ***L.E.A.D. Like You Mean It*™** - Overwhelmed by the current economic climate and its impact on your business? By low employee morale? By stagnant recruiting of top talent? By having to do more with less – less time, money, and people? Learn the 4 L.E.A.D. principles necessary to build a solid foundation from which to leap to the next level. These principles get to the core of personal leadership which influences your ability to make authentic connections consciously.
2. ***The 5 Worst Workplace Mistakes That Will Stop You Dead in Your Tracks*** – Each day your managers are creating the future of your organization. Are they leaving the kind of legacy you can be proud of? Discover the worst manager mistakes – and how to avoid them – to become an effective leader that produces results while building team relationships.
3. ***An Unforgettable Flight: From Huge Loss to Huge Gain*** – After losing both her father and brother in separate plane crashes, Marjorie's world collapsed in the blink of an eye… twice. Tragedies affect us in different ways, and when the unthinkable happens are you ready to cope? Pain is an inevitable part of life but how you handle it is a choice you can make.

Call for speaking fees and details on how you can receive complimentary copies of Marjorie's book, "My Road Back to Joy" or "The 78 Biggest Mistakes New Managers Make – What You Need to Know to Avoid Career Suicide."

www.TeamFusion.net

marjorie@teamfusion.net | 414-477-6655 phone | 414-386-1717 fax

For readers of
THE 78 BIGGEST MISTAKES NEW MANAGERS MAKE

VISIT WWW.78MANAGERMISTAKES.COM

Check out the FREE RESOURCES tab to select your additional bonuses!

You'll be able to download:
- My Favorites template
- The Art of Communication e-book
- The Art of Risk and Motivation e-book
- Presentation Checklist
- Manager Email Checklist
- And More!

NOTES

NOTES

NOTES

NOTES

NOTES

NOTES